Creative Non-Fiction

3 Manuscripts in 1 Book, Including: How to Write Non-Fiction, How to Self-Publish and How to Write Sales Copy

Jaiden Pemton

More by Jaiden Pemton

Discover all books from the Creative Writing Series by Jaiden Pemton at:

bit.ly/jaiden-pemton

Book 1: *How to Write Fiction*

Book 2: *How to Tell a Story*

Book 3: *How to Write a Screenplay*

Book 4: *How to Write Sales Copy*

Book 5: *How to Edit Writing*

Book 6: *How to Self-Publish*

Book 7: *How to Write Non-Fiction*

Book 8: *How to Write Content*

Themed book bundles available at discounted prices:

bit.ly/jaiden-pemton

Copyright

Table of Contents

Book 1: How to Write Non-Fiction

7 Easy Steps to Master Creative Non-Fiction, Memoir Writing, Travel Writing & Essay Writing

Jaiden Pemton

Introduction

Welcome to "How to Write Non-Fiction". In this guide, we are going to explore how to create an exciting and engaging narrative that will captivate your readers. In particular, we are going to discuss how you can write effectively so that your readers can find your content easily digestible.

You see, the difference between good writing, and great writing, is in the way you get your message across. Many times, getting your message across is about putting yourself in your reader's shoes. When you do this, you're able to transport your readers straight into your state of mind. This is what creates an authentic reading experience.

Now, most people believe that writing non-fiction is about using academic-style prose. As such, the aim is to sound smart. This is why many non-fiction writers try their hardest to sound as smart as they can. However, this is a misconception. You don't need to sound "smart" to be a successful non-fiction writer. All you need to do is transmit the enthusiasm you have for your chosen topic. Then, you can create compelling writing that will leave readers wanting more.

In each of the chapters in this guide, we'll look at a major step in the creative writing process. It's important to note that each step builds on the previous one. In the end, you will have a winning formula once you put them all together. You will learn a successful system that has been proven to work time and time again.

So, what are you waiting for?

Let's get started with this journey into a world filled with exciting moments. After all, writing should be an enjoyable process. It should be the type of endeavor that will leave you feeling happy and satisfied with the type of content you are able to produce. Plus, you surely have something to share with the world.

That's what makes writing such a rewarding experience.

Please don't look at writing as a job. If you do so, it will become a chore, a burden if you will. As such, please take the time to go through each of the steps in this guide. You will find that writing will become one of the most rewarding and satisfying experiences you can even engage in.

Please bear in mind that the most successful writers are the ones who can convey their passion for a given topic. This passion is transmitted through their keen sense of communicating their thoughts and ideas. The best part is that this is a skill that can be developed. Therefore, anyone can develop the skills needed to be a successful writer.

Happy writing!

Chapter 1: Step 1 - Deciding on Your Narrative

All great books tell a story. Now, you might think that type of approach is reserved for fiction writing. After all, fiction is, by definition, telling a story. While this is completely true, you will find that telling a story is not just reserved for fiction. Non-fiction works can also tell a story. In fact, non-fiction writing should tell a story. The reason for this is the need for creating a narrative.

When you write in the non-fiction domain, you must strive to create a consistent narrative that can deliver meaning and value to readers in an enjoyable format. This implies that you must avoid sterile discussions. Such discussions leave readers lacking a personal touch throughout the content. Therefore, it is essential for you to find a consistent narrative that reflects your true self.

In this chapter, we are going to look at the elements you need to create a consistent narrative that will enable you to engage readers in such a way that your content resonates with them. Best of all, you will find that you don't need exceptional skills to make this type of approach perfectly plausible.

Finding Your True Voice

Often, you hear writing coaches tell their students they need to find their true voice. However, that is vague, especially if you don't know how to bring your inner voice out. Finding your inner voice is about channeling your personality. When writing, you don't need to pretend to be someone you're not.

This is one of the biggest mistakes that novice writers make.

You see, novice writers attempt to sound smart and sophisticated. This approach leads them to labor through writing tasks as they search for complex vocabulary and grammatical structures. The truth is that readers don't expect to find uber-complex language when they pick up a book. In fact, many readers simply want an enjoyable read that will leave them with the information they seek.

Here is a great exercise you can do to help you find your voice.

When you set out to write on any given topic, sit down, and write. Just write. Don't think about what others will think. Just write down your ideas. You can write as much or as little as you like. A good starting point on one page.

Once you've written your first page, stop and read it. When you read it, you will get a glimpse of the way you sound, that is, your inner voice. Of course, you would have to clean it up. After all, it is extremely rare for a writer to produce flawless content on the first try. The aim here is to simply become comfortable with your own voice.

Then, take the time to write more and more. As you write, pay attention to the type of words you use. Also, check out the type of sentences you build. You will immediately find a consistent pattern. This is your voice. As you uncover your voice, you will need to take care of appropriate grammar, spelling, and vocabulary. This is especially important if you're writing on a technical topic.

These first few pages may never see the light of day. They may remain filed away in your computer forever. However, they are the beginning of your journey as a writer. They will serve to help you find your voice. The most important thing to keep in mind is that you're not writing to please others. You're writing to get a message across.

All About Grammar, Spelling, and Vocabulary

Letting your hair down is a major step toward becoming a successful writer. However, you must ensure that you follow the proper grammatical guidelines of the English language. Of course, there is a place for certain devices such as the use of slang or informal expressions. Nevertheless, you must ensure that you use the proper vocabulary and expressions you need based on your chosen topic.

When it comes to grammar, it is important to make sure that you're using the right verb tense and sentence structure. Please keep this in mind as grammatical mistakes are the first thing that people will call you out on. Such mistakes might turn off some readers. Others may dismiss your writing entirely. While it is possible to have a mistake at some point, too many mistakes will definitely get you in trouble.

So, it's a good idea to enlist the help of an editor. You can get a trusted friend or family member to go over your writing. If you would rather get an objective third-party, you can hire a freelance editor to give your writing a look. You can find them on sites such as Fiverr. Also, you can use editing software to double-check your work. In the end, the software can help you pinpoint mistakes that you may not have caught.

As for spelling, word processing software generally checks this for you on the fly. As such, you can rely on your word processor of choice to give you a hand. In case you in doubt, a good old-fashioned dictionary will come in handy. Often, there are words and terms that even sophisticated software does recognize. So, it makes sense to have a handy reference guide. That way, you can be sure that you're getting the right spelling. If you happen to use words from other languages such as Latin or Greek, always take the time to double-check the terms. That way, you can be sure you're right on the mark.

Regarding vocabulary, please ensure that you have the right terminology. This is particularly important if you're writing on a technical subject. Often, there are specific terms that you may not be sure about. Also, things might get confusing with definitions. As such, it's always good to review that you're using the right definitions and interpretations of words.

Finding the Right Pace

Non-fiction writing can be tricky in terms of pacing. It can be quite tough to find an appropriate pace. After all, you run the risk of moving along too fast or moving along too slowly. When you fail to find the appropriate pace, readers may feel they are not getting their money's worth.

Think about it along with these terms.

In non-fiction writing, it is essential that you get to the point. Sure, you can write short introductions to present the topic. However, the sooner you get to the point, the better. When you're exploring a specific topic, the last thing you want is to drag out explanations and descriptions. Often, it's best to limit the length of definitions and focus more on examples. Also, descriptions need to be as concise as possible.

The biggest temptation here is to provide lengthy and elaborate explanations. While providing details is certainly useful, there is a limit to the level of detail you need to provide. Granted, there are topics that require a high degree of detail. In such cases, your experience and intuition will tell you how detailed you need to be. After all, you're the expert on the topic. Nevertheless, it's always best to keep things as simple as possible.

It is also important to consider your audience. Depending on the people you're writing for, you might need to slow down or speed up. For example, if you're writing a guide for beginners, you might want to slow things down and provide a greater level of detail. If you're writing a guide for experienced users, then you can certainly move along quicker.

A good rule of thumb here is to check out other books and content similar to what you are looking to produce. By comparing these other materials, you can get an idea of what works and what doesn't. That can provide you a good yardstick by which to measure your own writing. In the end, there is nothing wrong with drawing comparisons when you're new to writing.

Over time, your experience and intuition will provide you with the proper feel for the pacing you need to keep throughout your book. Moreover, you'll know where to slow down, when to pick things up, and when to really drill down.

Please bear in mind that your inner voice should make itself manifest. This means that your voice will be the reflection of your knowledge and experience. Ultimately, you can provide readers with an adequate sense of your mastery of the topic. That will produce a sense of security among your readers. They will come to recognize you as an authority on the subject.

Maintaining a Consistent Narrative

Please keep in mind that building a consistent narrative is essential in successful writing. For example, if you have a clear position on an issue, make sure you maintain this position. Flip-flopping on issues will most likely confuse your readers.

When you write guides or how-to materials, it's always a good idea to maintain consistent use of tone, grammar, vocabulary, and pacing. For instance, using complex vocabulary with an academic tone at the beginning of the book and then shifting to an informal tone with the use of slang, later on, will serve to create an inconsistent dynamic in your book. Therefore, maintaining a consistent narrative through your materials will lead readers to feel comfortable with your writing. In the end, they will come to trust you as they get a clear glimpse into your psyche. Ultimately, this will create the right environment for the materials you want to present to your readers.

Chapter 2: Step 2 – Defining Your Purpose

When setting out to write, you must find your purpose. There must be a clear purpose for your writing. Otherwise, your content might come off as a rant with no clear direction. Naturally, that's the last thing you want to get across. Therefore, your writing needs to convey a clear message. When you do that, your readers will derive value from your words. In the end, your writing becomes a valuable source of knowledge and information.

In this chapter, we are going to look at finding your purpose. This is one of the most crucial elements any time you set out to write. When you have a clear purpose, writing becomes that much easier. As such, your inner voice will manage to find its way through to your audience in a clear and easy-to-follow manner.

How to Find Your Purpose

The first question you need to ask yourself is "why?" Generally speaking, you need to ask yourself why you are setting out to write. The answer to this question will reveal the type of approach you need to take. For example, some professionals set out to write a book as a means of positioning themselves in their chosen profession. Others write because they feel it's a way of letting their feelings out. Others write because they feel passionate about an issue. Therefore, they feel that writing about that issue will raise awareness of it.

Regardless of your specific purpose, you must ask yourself why you want to write in the first place. From there, you can derive the approach you need to get your message across. Consequently, your message is the second step in this process. You must ask yourself what your message is. This concept boils down to figuring out what you want your readers to take away from your materials.

Once you have your purpose and message clearly defined, the last step is to determine your audience. This is essential as the tone of your writing needs to reflect your audience. Naturally, writing for a younger audience would require you to use a more youthful and informal tone. In contrast, writing for an older audience would require a more formal tone.

Ultimately, your approach will depend on all three factors outlined here. By taking the time to think about them thoroughly, you will make the actual writing process easier for you.

Types of Purposes

There are different types of purposes for writing. Understanding them will give you a good idea of what approach you can take. So, let's discuss them in greater detail.

Writing to Inform

This is the type of writing you can use to present information on any given topic. When you write to inform, you are simply presenting facts and information. For example, you can write a how-to guide, describe historical events, or simply discuss an issue. Ultimately, you want to maintain a neutral position, especially if you want to spark debate among readers.

Writing to inform is also about making sure you get the fact straight. Therefore, accurate information is a must. This also means getting definitions and terms right. Moreover, you want to make sure that you know your audience. That way, you can tailor your style to suit the age and background of your readers.

Writing to Persuade

There are times when you write to get a specific point across. In such cases, your point might be to persuade your readers on a position in a given issue. Thus, you need to present a convincing argument based on the facts you present. Generally speaking, writing to persuade requires an engaging tone that's meant to awaken your reader's interest. In this type of writing, using creative descriptions is always best. Having a deep level of detail is essential to defeating any qualms your readers might have. In the end, your argument is so convincing that readers will be swayed in your direction.

Writing to Raise Awareness

When you write to raise awareness on an issue, you need to communicate a specific sense of urgency. There are cases in which you want to address an extremely urgent matter. Hence, you need to cut straight to the chase. Very little introduction or background is needed. What readers expect in such cases is a quick rundown of facts. These facts are intended to highlight your position. As such, there will be no denying the importance of the issue you discuss. Here, a quick, fast-paced approach is a must.

Writing to Advertise

Some materials are intended to advertise a product or service. With these materials, it's important to underscore a problem and then show how the product or service provides a solution. Often, companies write books and papers on the most pressing issues for their customers. Then, products and services are presented as a solution to these issues. In the end, the company closes with a call to action. Readers are then compelled to learn more about the company's solutions to their problems. This type of writing needs to be persuasive and filled with actionable information readers can use to find a solution to their needs.

As you can see, the various types of writing can help you create valuable materials. Depending on your specific purpose, you might end up with a combination of all of these approaches. The main thing to keep in mind is your main purpose and the message you're looking to get across.

Getting the Right Message Across

All too often, writers get sidetracked and lose sight of their message. As such, it is essential that you keep your eyes on the prize at all times. Once you define what your message is, you need to make sure that comes across.

Let's look at an example.

You're a professional that aims to write a white paper outlining your customers' biggest problems. Therefore, your purpose is to inform, but also to advertise. As such, you want to list your customers' problems in a clear and direct manner. Something like a "top 5" or the "Three Biggest Problems" works very well to pique readers' interest. As you go through each problem, the idea is to be neutral. You want to avoid creating a negative feeling in the mind of your customers. If you do, they won't look at your products as a solution. They will look at your products as a result of the problem.

Next, outline how your product can help your customers solve their problems. Now, you want to be careful not to make any outrageous claims. But you do want to present your argument in a way that all readers can see the benefits of your product. Here, you want to provide a solid level of detail. That way, the virtues of your product will become evident.

Lastly, close out with a call to action. Something like, "visit our website to learn more" is a great way of moving from an informative approach to a selling one. In the end, your readers will find value in the information you provide, while also leading them to purchase your products.

In this example, we have a combination of writing to inform and persuade. Naturally, you want your readers to purchase your product. However, keeping a neutral and informative tone is a great way of helping your future customers see the value of your products. Otherwise, you might turn some customers off if they see you're simply peddling something.

Always Stay Positive

Keeping a positive attitude is always critical. Even if you're dealing with serious issues like climate change, you still want to maintain a positive mindset. Sure, it's important to stress the importance of serious issues. Nevertheless, attempting to evoke fear or outrage in our audience will only take you so far.

Think about this situation.

A pest control company writes a brochure about their services. The company goes on about how termites can destroy a house. If customers don't act quickly, pests might bring their house crashing down.

On the surface, that looks like effective marketing. However, customers may seek this company out of fear. In the end, customers will associate the company with a negative feeling. To maintain a positive attitude, the company can list the dangers that termites pose to a house. As such, the company is the leading source for pest control services. Ultimately, this company has the solution to any type of problem.

Do you see the difference?

The aim is to inform you about a problem by listing the potential dangers. The idea is to provide accurate information and not create panic. Then, the company presents its services as the ultimate solution to the problem. As a result, the company is associated with a solution and not the result of a terrible situation.

Please keep in mind that maintaining a positive attitude at all times is the best way for you to ensure that you're writing is always associated with positive feelings. Unless you're writing a horror novel, you should always strive to have your readers associate your content with positive feelings. This will ensure that your readers get valuable information while you position yourself as a leading source in your chose field. That's the best approach you can use to keep your readers on your side.

Chapter 3: Step 3 - Determining your Audience

A critical aspect of effective writing knowing who will read your materials. Successful writers are keen on adapting their writing style to suit whomever their intended audience is. This makes it easier for them to communicate with readers.

Knowing who your audience depends on a few key factors. That is why this chapter is all about determining what your audience is. Moreover, you will find that once you figure out who your audience is, you can tweak your style as needed.

So, let's jump right into it!

It Starts with the Topic

The starting point should always be your topic. The topic itself will tell you quite a bit about the audience you'll be catering to. This is important to note as not everyone is interested in the same topics. For example, if you're writing a knitting guide, chances are you're not going to attract many guys. By the same token, a car repair book would not attract too many ladies. Now, this isn't to say that these topics are gender exclusive. What we are saying is that certain topics cater to one specific group of people more than another.

Of course, there are cross-cutting topics that everyone would be interested in reading. For instance, books on saving money are always popular regardless of people's specific demographics. The point here is to ensure that that you have a good idea of who would be interested in reading your content.

Also, please keep in mind that some topics are considered "niche" topics. These topics cater to a very specific group of individuals. As such, these groups possess very clear characteristics that you need to consider. A good example of this is sports. While sports, as a whole, are generally quite popular, individual sports may become niche topics. After all, how many fans does curling have compared to soccer? These are considerations that you must take into account when determining your audience.

Age and Gender

One of the most important aspects to consider is age. Naturally, some topics are more attractive to younger people than to older folks, and vice-versa. You can figure out what topics folks are interested in by doing an online search. You can search for something like, "most popular books teens" to uncover what types of topics are trending among teenagers.

Also, going on online platforms such as Amazon can reveal what types of books are most popular. There, you can see the topics that most readers are into. That should give you an indication of the types of readers your content can resonate with.

As for gender, there are specific topics that resonate with males more than females and vice-versa. As such, some common sense can go a long way with this demographic. However, you might be surprised to find that some topics have cross-cutting appeal. These are topics that would interest people from all walks of life. Topics such as health and fitness, finance, and self-development all have cross-cutting appeal. Nevertheless, you will find more gender-specific topics even within the broader scope of such topics.

Tone and Approach

When putting pen to paper, your readers' level of education plays an important role in determining the type of prose you aim to utilize. In this regard, you need to determine if you're writing for a general audience or a more specific one. In the case of academic publications, you need to maintain a tone consistent with more complex and abstract language.

However, if you're writing for a general audience, you might want to keep a more standard tone. By the same token, general audiences appreciate a more neutral tone, that is, using gender-neutral pronouns while avoiding any direct references to specific characteristics otherwise required in the topic. For example, you can address your readers directly by saying "you," while avoiding gender-specific pronouns like "he" or "she." In such cases, you can opt for the use of "they."

A good rule of thumb to keep in mind is to sound as natural as possible. If you normally speak with a more laid-back tone, then that should be your default tone. Also, if you're more inclined to speak in a formal tone, then make sure you get that message across, too. The main idea here is to avoid trying to be someone you're not. Often, this is the biggest mistake that novice writers make in the early going. Your natural voice will surely resonate with your target audience quickly and easily.

Leveraging Social Media

Social media is the place to be now if you want to know what's in, and what's out. Being relatively active on social media can give you the opportunity to see what's trending. Also, you can stay up to date with the latest news and information. As such, you can leverage social media to get a great idea of how your potential readers react to specific situations.

If you already have a following, then social media is the best way for you to stay in touch with them. As you interact with your followers, you can get specific insight into who they are and what they are interested in. This is crucial when it comes to tailoring your style to suit their needs.

Fiction writers love to interact with their readers. In doing so, they can gain an understanding about readers' interests, expectations, and demands. Believe it or not, your readers will demand certain things from you. In some cases, these demands surrounding events or characters. In others, your readers may ask you to write about specific topics. This is especially true in the non-fiction domain.

Another great way that writers leverage social media is to ask their readers to suggest topics they would like to read about. This is a great way of giving people what they want. Many times, readers have specific questions they would like you to answer for them. If you can provide those answers, your readers will surely follow you. So, do take the time to interact with your readers on social media whenever possible.

Capitalizing on Trends

Every now and then, events occur that capture news headlines and most people's attention. These events permeate the social landscape for any given length of time. These are wonderful opportunities for you to write on issues most people are interested in.

When you look to capitalize on trends, you need to pick a position and run with it. For example, let's assume you're looking to write on a current political issue. You may choose to remain neutral and just inform on the matter. That's perfectly fine. However, you must ensure that you always remain neutral. On the other hand, you might choose to state your position and write from that perspective. Therefore, your writing would have to be geared toward those folks who subscribe to your specific position. That means using the type of language and tone that is consistent with those folks.

Also, you must consider the overall profile of your readers. For instance, if you're address trends more popular with younger audiences, then you need to keep and light, fast-paced approach. Please bear in mind that younger individuals may not have the luxury of sitting down to read a long article. By the same token, your work might be oriented toward older individuals. These folks may have more time to devote to reading. Therefore, you can afford to make your point more elaborately.

Please keep in mind that any time you address current events, you must try to stay on the cutting edge. Thus, it's crucial for you to ensure that you present information that's consistent with your readers' wishes and desires. Ultimately, the topic itself doesn't really matter. What does matter is the way that you present it to your audience?

Important Considerations

Whenever you set out to write, it's always a good idea to put yourself in your readers' position. After all, you need to produce content that people would actually like to read. Often, this means putting yourself on the other side of the ball. Always ask yourself, "why would anyone read this?" The answer to this question can serve as a means of producing relevant content.

It's important to learn from mistakes. If previous content wasn't successful, you need to figure out why it didn't take off. That analysis will enable you to make changes so that your readers can get what they expect. Ultimately, it's about meeting your readers' expectations consistently so that you can continue to gain momentum in your following.

Lastly, please keep in mind that your readers change over time. With changing trends and situations, you might find that a winning combination may need to be altered. Therefore, it's always a good idea to stay in touch with your audience. That way, you can find out what they need and how you can deliver it to them. This is why staying in touch with readers is always a great idea. Successful writers build email lists. Then, they encourage their readers to submit questions and any suggestions. In doing so, you can ensure a constant feedback loop that allows you to find a great way of discovering new topics to keep you relevant.

Please bear in mind that successful writers always deliver what their readers want. That's the bottom line. If you can do that, you will always have a winning combination regardless of the topic itself. In the end, you will engage your readers in such a way that your communication will only continue to get stronger.

Chapter 4: Step 4 - Outlining Chapters Effectively

Proper organization is critical when it comes to writing a great book. Many times, novice writers commit a huge mistake by not properly organizing their content. Organizing content is all about ensuring that you have an adequate pace and flow to the way the material is presented. In other words, you have an appropriate setup, thereby ensuring your readers will have no trouble following your lead.

The entire organization process begins with outlining chapters based on the amount of information you wish to cover. Naturally, larger books with more content will need more chapters than books with less content. As a result, you need to be aware of how many sections you need to break your book down into.

In this chapter, we are going to take a look at how you can organize your content effectively while ensuring the overall flow of the material.

Understanding the Scope of Your Project

The single most important thing you need to consider when starting your project is its scope. By "scope," we mean the amount of material that you wish to cover. For example, if you're looking to cover a good chunk of material, then you are looking at a broader scope. If you're looking to cover less content, then you are looking at a narrower scope.

Please bear in mind that it's quite easy to get sucked into pushing for a broader scope. This can happen if you're not disciplined enough to write up an outline and then stick to it. This generally occurs when writers don't have a clear sense of where they are going. This is why you must ensure that you have a clear idea of where you want your project to go.

Consider this situation:

You are writing a book on holiday decorations. At first, you wish to focus solely on Christmas decorations. Then, you realize that Halloween decorations are also fun to do. So, you add those to the book. After that, you figure that Easter decorations would also be good. And so, you keep adding to the book.

Now, there is nothing wrong with the amount of information you plan to include in your book. The problem is that you never had a clearly defined scope. As such, your book appears to be a collection of random items all mashed together. Perhaps a better approach would have been to create separate volumes. For instance, one volume would focus solely on Christmas decorations, then the second on Halloween, the third on Easter, and so on.

In this example, you will find that simply adding and adding to your book will create a mix of ideas that may not necessarily fit well together once joined. So, do make sure that you have the right scope in mind when setting out to write your book.

Outlining Chapters

Once you have determined your scope, that is how much you plan to cover, you can move on to breaking down your content into chapters. A chapter is essentially a very broad idea that you will develop. In this development, you can break down the idea into as much detail as possible given the constraints you have. These constraints are limited to time and space. As for time, you might be on a deadline. As such, writing too much can negatively affect the time you have to complete the project. The second constraint is space. For instance, you may be working with a specific number of words. Therefore, you can't afford to ramble on too much. Otherwise, you'll run out of words.

To outline your chapters, all you need to do is break down your topic into subtopics. Each subtopic represents the main idea about the topic. These main ideas are important pieces that must be put together in order to assemble the entire puzzle.

There are no specific rules or guidelines on how many chapters should be in a book or the specific word count. This decision is based on your expertise and experience as a writer. A good rule of thumb is to break your main topic into about three to five main ideas. From there, you can use them to plan each chapter.

Now that you have your chapters outlined, then you can go on to decide the actual content that will be included in the chapter. This is largely a tactical decision, meaning that you'll choose what to include and what not, once you're in the writing process. For instance, many writers choose to leave out specific content that isn't directly related to their overall idea. Others choose to add content that they have not thought of before.

Please bear in mind that this organization is not set in stone. However, you must try your best to stick to your original plan as much as possible. That way, you can reduce the amount of wasted time spent on a topic.

How to Determine What Stays and What Goes

As mentioned earlier, the actual words you write in each chapter are a game-time decision. Some writers like to be very detailed. As such, they outline everything that will be included in the chapter. Others are less proactive. So, they don't actually plan out everything that will go into the chapter. They just sit down and write. It should be noted that you can get away with this when you're an experienced writer. If you're not that experienced in the topic itself, you can use other books on a similar subject as a starting point.

As you write, you may find that some ideas don't mesh well with the topic or other chapters in the book. So, you may choose to eliminate it from the book. Additionally, you may choose to deviate from your plan. This means that your instincts and knowledge will help you determine what to keep and what not.

Once you are satisfied with the direction a chapter has taken, you can review it to ensure it represents your idea. If needed, changes can improve the chapter. Otherwise, leaving the chapter as is, will help you move on. The aim is to progress as much as possible.

Figuring Out Your Word Count

This is one of the most common questions novice writers encounter. Determining the word count for a book is not always easy. However, there are parameters that you can follow. For example, a 5,000-word book is like a quick guide. At first, 5,000 might sound like a lot, but the reality is that it is not.

Additionally, a 10,000-word book is suitable for an introduction to a topic. Books ranging from 10,000 to 20,000 words offer a good level of detail into a specific topic. Books with a 20,000-to-30,000-word count are rather complex books. They generally require more content given their word count. Anything above 30,000 words is a voluminous book. At this level, you may have to really broaden your scope, or break down the topic into a very high level of detail. In the end, this level of detail will enable you to take up space you need to fully discuss the outcome.

Another good way of figuring out your word count is by looking at other similar books on the same topic. The size of the book can give you an adequate indication of how many words you might need to cover your ideas.

Sketching your Outline

Now that you have your chapters and content figured out, it's time to draft up your outline. Having an outline is essential to writing a book as soon as possible, and as accurately as possible. While it's true the some of the best writers are poor organizers, the fact is that you can't afford to be sloppy. As you gain more experience, you might be able to get past this limitation. However, novice writers would do well to write their outline.

A simple organization scheme can be using numerals for chapter numbers and bullet points for the subtopics. Then, you can consult your outline as you progress through the content. This is an important point as having a clear path for your book will lead you to successfully complete it.

Consider this sample outline:

1. Chapter 1: Introduction to the Stock Market
   a. Definition of the stock market
   b. Types of markets
   c. Products traded on the stock market
   d. People involved in the stock market

In this sample outline, we defined one chapter with four subtopics. The next step is to figure out the word count. You can do this by determining how much detail you wish to provide. If you aim to provide only general ideas, then 1,000 words might be enough for this chapter. However, if you want to really dig deep into the subject, you might find that 2,000 to 3,000 words might be more than enough.

You can follow this same system for all chapters in your book. In the end, you'll have a neatly polished outline for your book. It is often said that with a good outline, a book writes itself. This is true because having a good outline eliminates guesswork. As such, all you have to worry about is writing down the information you wish to communicate.

So, please take the time to think about how much content you wish to cover and how you intend to break it down. Doing this will save you time and headaches further down the road.

Chapter 5: Step 5 - Establishing Credibility Through Research

In the non-fiction world, credibility is crucial. After all, you cannot expect to be taken seriously if you're not careful with the information you put forth. Often, publishers and writers make sensationalist claims just to sell more books. However, these claims, if unfounded, can land you in serious trouble. Nevermind that your books won't sell, you can get sued. Therefore, it is important to conduct research effectively. That way, you can use these sources to back up any claims that you make as part of your publications.

When conducting research, it's a good idea to use the best practices implemented by academic writers. In academic writing, virtually everything you say must be backed up by some kind of credible source. This is why becoming familiar with research sites and other mainstream publications is a must. Moreover, you cannot expect to be taken seriously if you cite sources from non-credible sources. These sources include private individuals not considered experts, fringe organizations, or any other type of non-respected source.

In this chapter, we are going to take a look at how you can use research and trusted sources to boost your publications' credibility.

Not All Sources Are Created Equal

When looking at sources, it's often a question of common sense. For starters, there are organizations and institutions which are widely respected. For example, universities, international institutions, and official government organizations are all sources you can rely on. By citing information from these sources, you can back up the claims that you make in your works.

Perhaps the hardest part of conducting research is gaining access to these sources. This can be a challenge if you don't know where to look. So, let's take a look at the places where you can find the information you need.

- *Google Scholar*. This is the first stop for anyone looking to find credible sources on virtually any type of content. Google Scholar is a search engine that is dedicated specifically to finding academic articles published in major magazines and journals, while also offering books and articles.
- *Academic databases*. There are specific academic databases that are widely used by researchers. The best example of these is JSTOR. You can find a plethora of information there. However, please note that you may have to purchase a subscription to these databases if you want to have unlimited access.
- *Journals*. Most major fields of research have dedicated journals. These journals publish articles on topics related to

these fields of research. Since the vast majority of these journals are peer-reviewed, the publications in them are considered to be trustworthy. So, always search for journals on your chosen topic. Most back issues are freely available though you may have to purchase current editions.

- *Subject matter experts*. A subject matter expert is a respected individual who is recognized for their expertise in a given area. Citing them is a great way of making your points come alive. You can cite interviews, articles, and lectures given by these individuals. So, always check out who the relevant experts are in your specific subject.

- *Institutional information*. This type of information is generally posted by governments, international organizations, or private companies. Therefore, the information officially published by these institutions constitutes a real position you can use to back up your claims. For example, the United Nations publishes official positions on any number of subjects. As such, you can confidently use the United Nations as backing for the information you present.

Please bear in mind that virtually all of this information is freely available. So, all you have to do is take the time to do the research. While going to your local library still works well, you will find that using the power of the internet makes the research a lot faster and easier.

Using Disclaimers

Many writers use disclaimers as a means of warning readers that they are only publishing opinions and not making official recommendations. This is important, especially when you're not licensed to advise on a specific matter. For example, you can write a well-researched book on a health issue. However, if you're not a licensed practitioner in that field, you can get sued for the use readers make of that information. So, it's a good idea to include a disclaimer in which you free yourself of such responsibility.

Also, writers and publishers use disclaimers to make it known that the information they provide is for "entertainment purposes" only. Again, this type of disclaimer is widely used in areas that may constitute a risk for the publisher. So, it's always best to double-check if you need to include such disclaimers. A good rule of thumb is to include one whether you need it or not.

That being said, having a well-researched book will help you avoid being criticized for providing senseless information. As such, you can encourage readers to check out the sources you have presented. In that way, readers can take your analysis plus sources to derive their own conclusions.

Making Citations

Another important element to presenting your research is the use of citations. Depending on the nature of your publication, you can use simple citations such as, "according to…" or "in the opinion of…" These citations are used to introduce the source from which you have derived your information. Moreover, they are used in-text to inform the reader about where the information is coming from.

If you choose, you can use a specific citation format such as MLA, APA, or Vancouver. These types of citation methods are dependent on the type of content. For instance, MLA is used in most academic areas of research. Its defining characteristic is the use of footnotes at the bottom of the page. The APA format is the most used and can be implemented for any type of publication. The Vancouver citation method is mostly used within the medical sciences. Nevertheless, you can choose to use this format if it works best for you.

Ultimately, it's important to use a specific citation format, especially if you're looking to present a more academic paper. Most non-fiction books don't need such a level of detail. Nevertheless, it's always a good idea to put your best foot forward. This level of detail is used by professionals who are looking to position themselves as subject matter experts in their respective fields.

Being Careful with Plagiarism

Plagiarism is a sure-fire way of getting you banished from the face of the Earth. For instance, Amazon has very strict guidelines about how much duplicate content you can use. Generally speaking, you cannot upload a book that has more than 5% duplicate content. Therefore, a copy and paste approach is not going to cut it. While other platforms may let this slide, there is a very good chance you'll get called out on it eventually.

Plagiarism is considered fraud. While it may not get you in jail, it will automatically get you discredited. Once you are officially discredited, getting back into the good graces of readers is practically impossible. Therefore, you must be very careful about what information you use, and how you use it.

This is why the best way to go is to cite information that you use while limiting the use of direct quotes. Often, writers like to quote other speakers and writers directly. However, this may get you a strike for duplicate content. So, it's best to use direct quotes sparingly.

The best way to use information and quotes from other speakers and writers is to paraphrase. Paraphrasing means writing someone else's words in your own. For example, something like "in the words of Mark Twain…" can be a useful way of ensuring that you present the information you want without getting nailed for improper use.

Please bear in mind that plagiarism is the absolute worst thing you can do in the non-fiction world. So, it's best to ensure that you have the proper citations and give credit when it's due.

Working Around Plagiarism

Some unscrupulous folks simply rewrite other established materials. While this is perfectly legal, it's considered unethical. This is especially important if you're serious about positioning yourself within your respective field. There is nothing wrong with paraphrasing other stuff. Just make sure you follow proper citation guidelines.

Now, let's assume that you simply rewrite other material and publish under a pen name. That will do the trick. However, you will quickly find that most readers will catch on to your scheme. So, they may end up punishing you by leaving negative comments and bad reviews. Please keep in mind that bad comments are just as bad as being exposed to academic fraud. As such, ensuring that you always produce the best possible material is a must.

Lastly, please ensure that other writers you work with are on the same page as you are. While you will surely adhere to proper guidelines, you may not be so sure about others. If you suspect that other writers are fudging the rules, please make sure to call them out on it. If you fail to do so, your reputation may get tainted through no fault of your own.

Chapter 6: Step 6 - Understanding Subgenre

Genre is often at the center of discussion regarding successful non-fiction writing. Mainly, the discussion centers on getting the genre right. While that may seem relatively obvious, it isn't quite as straightforward as you might think. Defining a genre can be tough, especially if you're new to writing.

To define your book's genre, you must be first clear about what you're going to write. This is a crucial first step in determining your book's genre. Next, you need to have a clear vision of your book's scope. From there, you can safely determine your genre. Of course, that is easier said than done.

So, let's take a look at how you can define your book's genre and subgenre accurately. Best of all, you'll find that it's much easier than you think.

What Is Genre?

In essence, genre refers to the main topic of a book. This implies that you must have a clear sense of what your book is about. Now, in this book, we're dealing with one main, overarching genre which is non-fiction. As such, your book would most likely fall under the non-fiction genre.

While that's a great start, it's worth noting that such a description is too broad. Therefore, we must dig a little deeper and refine your book's genre and subgenre.

It's also important to note that genre encompasses rather extensive topics. These topics may cover a lot of different aspects. Yet, these are the main topics that readers will look for. From there, they may narrow down their search. This is why first appealing to a broad audience is key. From there, you can narrow your book's focus.

Please bear in mind that your book's genre should be reflected in its title. After all, your book's title will lead readers to find your content. So, you must make sure to include all the relevant words in the title. It will just make it easier for readers to find your work.

What Is Subgenre?

A subgenre is a narrower breakdown of your book's topic. In essence, it is the result of further refining your content. When you refine your content further down, you can come up with some rather specific topics to cover. As a result, you must ensure that your overall topic encompasses a clear subgenre.

Main topics such as knitting, gardening, personal finance, or home decoration are all too broad. Therefore, you must narrow your book's focus down to a clear perspective. This is why understanding your book's scope is so important. When you have a clear scope, then it's feasible for you to really drill down on the content you wish to cover.

Please keep in mind that the biggest mistake most novice writers make is leaving their scope too broad. Therefore, they have a tough time focusing on what they really want to say. If anything, they may find themselves bouncing all over the place. When that happens, there is no telling where the book may end up. This is why many writers begin working on a book, but never finish it.

Reflecting Genre and Subgenre in Your Book's Title

When selecting your book title, you must ensure that your genre and subgenres are adequately portrayed. In that regard, it can make an enormous difference between having a successful publication and a subpar one.

Consider this situation:

You have just completed a book on living room design. So, you choose to title it, "The Ultimate Living Room." This title is good, but it's a little too vague. Yes, you're reflecting on the fact that the book is about a living room. However, it doesn't tell the reader much more than that. Therefore, the book title doesn't make much sense.

In this case, a better title would be, "The Ultimate Living Room: 25 Great Decoration Ideas for a Small Budget." This title, while longer, encompasses everything you are looking to explain in this book. As such, any reader that comes across your book will know exactly what to expect. Consequently, this book title is much more effective when compared to the first one.

Please keep in mind that your clear understanding of your genre and subgenre must be stated in the title. Given the fact that there is a number of books on any number of topics, you need to make sure that yours stands out as much as possible. The best way to do this is by being absolutely clear about your genre in the title.

Improving Searchability

When you have a clearly defined genre, subgenre, and title, you drastically improve searchability. This is key regardless of the platform on which you sell your books. For example, if you sell your books on Amazon Kindle, readers search for topics based on keywords. These keywords are representative of the topic they are looking to read about. As such, you need to make sure that you have the right type of context in mind.

Now, the use of keywords is always important when looking to boost your book's marketing and sales. Keywords must therefore be used within the title. In the previous example, we were clear about including the terms "living room," "decoration," and "ideas."

Why?

Think about it for a minute.

Chances are that a reader would search for a book on this topic under the terms "living decoration ideas." In that case, you would have a clearly defined search. If your title represents these search terms, then you have automatically improved your book's chances of being discovered.

This is also true if you're selling your materials on your website. Your title can be discovered by Google. Therefore, it must reflect your genre and subgenre appropriately. This, in turn, will give search engines the opportunity to find your content amid tons of other types of content and materials.

Experienced writers know that visibility is paramount to successful content. By improving your searchability, you give your content a fighting chance to stand out. What searchability does is give your content a chance to shine through. Therefore, you have the opportunity to become successful based on your merits. Otherwise, great content may get lost in the shuffle. Needless to say, that is the last thing you want.

Thinking Big

When you have a clear idea of your genre, you can potentially break it up into an endless number of subgenres. This is important when looking at the bigger picture. The reason for this is based on the fact that you can create an entire series of books based on a general topic. From there, any number of specific subgenres can help you provide all types of readers options to choose from.

Let's consider this example.

You plan to write a series of books and sales and market. Since this is a broad topic, there are potentially endless types of books you could write. So, your job now becomes too narrow things down. For example, you could write a five-part series focused on sales and marketing for small businesses, startups, solopreneurs, online businesses, and family companies.

In this example, you took a broad topic, sales, and marketing, and then broke it down into five more specific topics. In the end, you were able to make the topic work effectively by creating a series of books. Now, instead of having one large volume divided into five parts, you have five separate volumes.

What's the advantage here?

The advantage is that you can boost your sales by appealing to a broader customer base, offering more selections, and focusing on specific market niches. For instance, a person who is interested in sales and market for small businesses would be interested in purchasing the volume dedicated to that topic. In contrast, if you had one volume with five topics, that interested reader may pass as your book contains topics they are not interested in.

Do you see how powerful this approach can be?

Ultimately, your goal is to leverage your writing skills so you can produce a greater income. In the end, you can do that with the same amount of effort. The only difference is that you are using your talents in a much more productive way.

Please keep in mind that you need to have a pretty good idea as to the genre and subgenre of your content even before you write a single word. While it is certainly possible that things can change along the way, it's also important to keep in mind that having a clear starting point can make the difference between a successful book and a disappointing one.

There is no question that you have what it takes to produce highly successful content. So, it's a question of focusing it appropriately. In that case, it will make your job that much easier. That's why it's important to give yourself a hand. Rather than make things harder than they have to be, you can improve your chances right from the start. So, make sure you have a clearly defined genre, subgenre, and title. When you put them all together, you'll have a recipe for a successful book or even a series of books.

Chapter 7: Step 7 - Building a Winning Formula

At this point, we have laid out the groundwork needed to build a winning formula. This winning formula is about developing a system that can help you become the most successful writer that you can.

Now, it's important to note that this isn't a magic formula. As such, this isn't something you can pull out of a box and let it roll. This winning formula is a highly personalized one. This means that you need to develop a keen understanding of the various elements discussed in this guide. From there, you can create a system that will help you deliver successful content time and time again.

So, we are going to dedicate this chapter to bringing everything together so that you can build a personal winning formula. From there, you will discover just how effective writing can truly be.

Playing to Your Strengths

This is pivotal. All writers have personal wheelhouse. That means there are topics and content that they are much better at than others. Therefore, play to your strengths, especially in the early going.

As you make a name for yourself, you want to put your best foot forward. As such, playing to your strengths makes perfect sense. For example, if you're a finance expert, then go down that path. Sure, it might be really exciting to think about writing the next great novel. However, the idea here is to build momentum. By building your momentum, you build your self-confidence. That is what gives you the ability to branch outside your comfort zone.

Also, please keep in mind that readers want value as much as possible. So, using your area of expertise to its fullest potential makes sense. Doing so will put you in a position of strength. In contrast, branching out into other areas may put you in a tough spot. So, playing to your strengths is always the best approach.

With time, you can venture outside the box. You can try working on other topics that you have always wanted to. By then, you'll already have a strong foundation beneath you. Consequently, you'll have the confidence to help you put your best foot forward. As a writer, your experience will help you figure out what works and what doesn't.

So, don't be afraid to go on the power play early on. Eventually, you'll have the experience you need to try new things out.

Use Your Voice

Throughout this guide, we've talked about being yourself. This is so true, especially when you're playing to your strengths. Using your voice is crucial when it comes to building rapport with your readers. Believe it or not, readers can pick up when you're trying to be someone you're not. Readers can tell by the way the words flow or don't.

You see, writing is a skill that is honed over time. It's part of an author's thought process. So, the challenge in writing is to organize your thought process in such a way that it's logical and coherent. That will lead readers down a path they can fully comprehend.

It's also important to keep in mind that inexperienced writers tend to produce well-written, but disjointed and incoherent text. Therefore, the challenge becomes to articulate your ideas clearly.

How can you articulate your arguments?

Use your outline!

Yes, when you use your outline, you can produce high-quality content that can lead you to focus your thoughts clearly and coherently. An outline helps you narrow your scope while keeping you on track. Otherwise, you run the risk of simply ranting on about personal experiences or things you know about. While this is useful to a certain degree, all successful books need to have a clear narrative.

Of course, you might hear some writers saying that sticking to outlines can be highly restrictive. That is true to some extent. It requires a lot of experience to simply write without any kind of formal outline, concept, and objective. As you gain experience, it's always a good idea to have a clearly defined concept.

One other thing. Please avoid trying to do everything in your head. When you try to do everything in your head, thoughts can often get muddled and confused. This can lead you to get stuck at any point in your book. So, make sure you write everything down. While it is totally possible to make changes, keeping a written record helps you establish the path you wish to take your readers on. Think of it as building a roadmap before setting out on your journey.

Stick to a Specific Narrative

There are some truly gifted writers out there. They can produce quality content on a number of topics. They can write about practically anything. That's both blessing and a curse.

You see, writers often become known for a specific type of genre. Think about all of the great fiction writers. They end up getting typecast into a specific genre because they are successful in it. As such, they focus their energy on that genre. After a while, they don't venture out into other genres, not because they don't have the talent, but to avoid confusing readers.

For instance, let's assume you have made a name for yourself in the medical field. People know you as a great health care professional. Naturally, people would be happy to see you produce content on health and wellness. Over time, you gain quite a bit of traction in this field. Then, you realize your lifelong dream of writing a novel. However, your readers are confused. You're known as a great healthcare professional. So, why are you writing a novel?

Do you see the point in this argument?

Now, it should be noted that lots of folks decide to make a 180-degree turn and write a novel. Also, some folks choose to write about topics they love. That's all well and good. The point is to choose a topic and run with it. Who knows, this could truly put you on the map.

Once you make a name for yourself, you must then commit to that genre. That way, your popularity, and success can just compound with each piece of content you publish. Eventually, you'll have the right following around you.

Branching Out into Other Genres

So, what if you can write about other genres?

In that case, it's best to go with a pen name. This is what all great writers do. You see, once a writer becomes known for a specific genre, they have no choice but to go with it. That's why adopting a pen name makes sense.

By taking on another personality, you can ensure that readers will not be biased by your previous success. In fact, some readers may be skeptical about your ability to be successful in other topics. Therefore, using a pen name can remove that bias from your readers' minds.

There is one significant upside to using a pen name. If for some reason, your content flops, your usual reputation won't take a hit. In a way, this takes the pressure off writing new content. For instance, if your first novel flops, you can simply learn from the mistakes. As such, it won't count against your current standing with your followers. This is one of the biggest advantages that writing offers good authors.

The downside to this is that you'll be practically starting from scratch. Your new persona won't have any kind of following. Therefore, you'll need to put in the time and effort to properly market your new content. Nevertheless, your previous experience can help you market your new content effectively.

As your new genre gains momentum, please keep in mind that you may need to eventually come out as the genius behind the magic. Nevertheless, you won't have to worry too much about that. Since your new content has gained popularity, readers will be impressed, not confused.

How Much Should You Write?

This question gets asked all the time. Many novice writers don't know how much they should write. Also, new authors don't have a sense of how often they should publish new material.

Well, there is a short and long answer to that question.

The short answer is that you should publish new material whenever you have it ready. This means that if it takes you six months to write a new book, then publish it then. Additionally, if it takes you two years to write one, then your audience will have to wait for you that long. Of course, you shouldn't take decades to come up with new material.

The long answer is that you should publish material when it's prudent to do so. For example, let's say that you published a highly successful book three months ago. Since you are a prolific author, you already have two more books in the final editing phase. So, you plan to publish as soon as the next one is ready.

That can be a mistake.

Why?

You see, successful authors publish new content until the sales of the previous ones have stalled. When sales stall, it means that everyone who wanted to read your book has already done it. So, it's time for something new.

Other writers like to follow a specific tempo. For instance, they publish a new book every six months, or once a year. If this sounds like you, it could be a good approach. After all, if your readers get used to your writing tempo, you may find yourself building a steady income stream.

In the end, your winning formula is about building a system that works for you based on good practices. You will find out what works for you soon enough. So, take the time to discover what works for you. Sometimes, you simply have to learn from your mistakes. However, the result will be totally worth it!

Conclusion

Thank you very much for taking the time to complete this guide. We hope that you now have a great sense of how to write non-fiction content. At this point, you should be able to understand how you wish to pursue your writing endeavors. Mainly, it's about ensuring that you have a system that can lead you to become a successful writer.

So, please take the time to go over any of the concepts provided in this guide. Repetition is a very important part of learning. As such, reviewing previous lessons is always a great way of ensuring that your knowledge has been fixated in your mind. Moreover, review and practice will help you become the best writer you can possibly be.

Often, developing great skills is a question of time. While we would all love to magically flip a switch, the fact is that most of the skills we learn in life come as the result of years of work and practice. Please keep the 10,000-hour rule in mind. This rule states that we need about 10,000 hours of practice before we can truly master a skill.

Now, does that mean that it will take you 10,000 hours to become a great writer?

Not necessarily.

What this idea means is that you need to put in the time and effort to become a successful writer. The more time and practice you put into your writing endeavors, the better you will get. Naturally, this approach means that your success is proportional to the amount of work and sacrifice you are willing to put in.

Please take this opportunity to truly allow your efforts to shine through. You already have the most important elements you need to be successful. So, it is just a matter of making your efforts become a testament to the hard work you are prepared to invest in. The difference between mediocre writers and great ones is the amount of effort and dedication put into their craft. The best writers in history were able to combine hard work and natural talent. Ultimately, this combination has led to some of the most famous works.

Good luck and happy writing!

Book 2: How to Self-Publish

7 Easy Steps to Master Self-Publishing, eBook Creation, Ghostwriting, Book Marketing & Publishing

Jaiden Pemton

Introduction

If you are starting with this guide, something has led you to consider self-publishing. You have probably heard of the liberation and total ownership of the self-publishing process, as well as the potential to earn more of your own money. If you are considering whether or how to take the leap into self-publishing, this guide is for you!

When it comes to self-publishing, you must be aware of the industry's ins and outs, the correct terminology to use, how to interact with editors, designers, your fans, network, and target audience, and potential retailers. In modern-day society, publishing is a more ambitious field than ever before, and you need to be on top of your game in order to thrive within it. Whether you're still wondering if self-publishing is for you, or you've already committed to the journey and just need to know where to go next, this guide will show you everything you need to know to thrive within the industry and make a name for yourself as a self-published author. Thank you for choosing to embark on this journey with us.

In order to be an effective self-publisher, you must be prepared to be thorough, intentional, and informed on every step of the journey. Self-publication requires an in-depth understanding of the industry, the genre you are writing in, how to check all the boxes in writing, editing, design, making necessary financial decisions, and marketing and distribution strategies to use.

With the writing industry becoming more challenging by the day, you must be willing to bring high energy to every step of the process. When you embark on the journey of self-publication, you must be clear-headed, driven in your goals, and ready to confront every logistic that comes your way. This guide will provide you with in-depth knowledge of each of these logistics, tactics for managing them, and how to keep your vision fresh in your mind throughout the process.

In this guide you will find a comprehensive step-by-step reference format with everything you need to know about the self-publication process. You will become familiar with the beginning and middle stages of the processes, as well as information to make marketing and distribution decisions at the end of the process. You will learn top secret tips and tricks for writing, editing, title generation, design, description writing, and publication logistics. You will understand how to use social media, build your fanbase, and maintain high audience engagement. Additionally, you will see easy-to-follow lists of key terms, secrets of success, and things to avoid.

The chapters of this guide will take you through each step of the self-publishing journey to help you check all of the necessary boxes and steer clear of any big mistakes. Each chapter is designed with astounding detail to help you stay on track and address any questions or concerns you have along the way. Regardless of where you're at on your self-publishing journey, this guide has all the tools you need to set yourself apart as an expert editor and is sure to serve as the perfect guide to revolutionize your editing experience.

Happy writing!

Chapter 1: Step 1 - The Basic Components of Self-Publishing

There are several significant differences between self-publishing and traditional publishing. Before you make a set decision on which route to choose, it is essential to consider the elements of both. Traditional Publishing requires the use of an agent, a publisher to accept your manuscript, and a contract between the publisher and yourself that allows the publisher to purchase rights to your book. After the publisher has purchased rights, they will assume responsibility for all further editing, formatting, and designing. The money you earn will be dependent on how well the book sells once it has hit the market.

Although you will have to pay less for production expenses and have fewer responsibilities in terms of the fine details, this process is highly competitive and can take a great deal of time. You can expect plenty of rejections from agents and publishers, and even if you land one, you may lose your sense of agency and creative input in how the final project turns out. This means that the book can be designed and edited without your input. In addition, if your book does do well, you will not earn as much as you could earn if you had self-published.

Benefits of Self-Publishing

Although self-publishing requires a lot of work in terms of editing, design, and distribution and may require more money upfront, it is an excellent option if you want to avoid the roadblocks of rejection, loss of agency in your book production, and potential loss of money once it hits the market. In many cases, self-publishing is a great place to start getting your name out there and building a fanbase surrounding your work.

Key Terminology

Once you've chosen to begin the self-publishing journey, there are a number of critical elements you need to be aware of. The most basic of these elements are publishing terms, which you should be prepared to interact with often throughout the publishing process. While you may not encounter all of these terms, it is essential to understand what they mean.

· Barcode → an image that indicates the ISBN and, in some cases, the book's price. Barcodes are machine-readable and are often used by book retailers on print books.

· Copyright → the declaration that the creator has exclusive rights to the publication, distribution, and adaptation of their work during a certain period of time.

· Description → the part of the book that communicates to distribution partners and, later, potential customers what the book is about and how to market it.

· Distributor → the party designated to credit, fulfillment, collections, and in the book industry, selling, on behalf of a publisher.

· E-Retailer → a book retailer who works in an online space.

· Edition → version of a book, many times which has been re-released with corrections or new features.

· ISBN (International Standard Book Number) → Aa13-digit code provided by the ISBN agency of a particular country and assumed by a publisher to demonstrate the format, edition, and publication details of a work. ISBNs are used globally and help to identify book titles and format information quickly.

· .jpg or jpeg. → image files that are most effective for colorful images to be used in the book.

· Keywords → single words or phrases which can be used to summarize the book and make it easier to search for.

· Metadata → necessary information about the book like the price, cover, publication date, author, description, table of contents, etc. which is used by booksellers and buyers.

· On Sale Date → the date when retail partners can start selling a book.

· Page Count → the total number of pages in a book (always divisible by two), including blank pages.

· PDF → Adobe file format which allows for easy creation and sharing of documents that are easy and consistent to print.

· Publication Date → the date a book can be released to retail consumers or libraries to assume possession of.

· Publisher → the person who owns legal rights to the book and makes decisions regarding when it will be available.

· Retailer → any place that sells books (sourced from publishers, distributors, and wholesalers) to consumers.

· Returns → the ability for booksellers to return books to the publisher if they have too many or no longer have use for a particular book. Booksellers must charge publishers the purchase price of the book and will then be reimbursed.

· Status → indicates whether or not a book is available, using terms like "forthcoming," "active," or "publication canceled".

· Subject → used to place books into categories based on content.

· Suggested Retail Price → indication of the price by the publisher.

· Title → information used for reporting and reseller catalog communications.

· Trade → traditional bookselling channels like independent and chain bookstores.

· Wholesaler → a business that is dedicated to fulfilling orders for retailers and libraries with the books they obtain from publishers and distributors.

Although self-publishing can be a taxing process, you can expect to fully control the content and design, marketing, and edits. Your book will likely have increased longevity because no one gets to decide when to stop marketing it. The royalties you save from having to pay a publisher can go into your own pocket instead, and you have the freedom to change the price of your book whenever you want.

Additionally, you have a greater ability to distribute the book worldwide and be in full control of the rights granted to foreign publishers who may want to purchase rights to distribute in their country. Lastly, self-publishing gives you a great deal of flexibility regarding your work timeline and the deals you cut with outside organizations. All in all, self-publishing is a great route for writers looking for independence, agency, and flexibility in their publishing process.

Chapter 2: Step 2 - Beginning Stages

The beginning stages of the self-publishing journey involves bringing your book into existence and getting the essential details underway. The three stages of this process are writing, editing, and generating a title. There are several tools available to help you throughout these processes.

Writing your Book

The first step of the self-publishing process is to write your book. Before you begin, you will need to determine the genre you are writing in. Consider the typical audience of this genre to decide who you are writing to. What kind of writing will pique their interest and keep them engaged? Be sure to pay attention to other relevant works in the genre, such as films, screenplays, and books by other authors, to inform yourself of what does best in the industry.

Writing from this place of understanding and inspiration can help you enjoy the process and ask yourself the critical question: *"What am I trying to say, and how can I say it in a way it hasn't been said before?"* You will need to take the necessary actions of character development, plot development, crafting setting, establishing style and voice, determining theme, making the experience personal, developing a shining moment, etc.

Before you begin to write, you should be able to narrow down what you are trying to say and what impact you want it to have on the readers. If you are writing a nonfiction book, you will need to carve out time to research your topic at great length to ensure credibility. If you are storytelling, you may need to experiment with various organizational techniques, central themes, points of view, and styles to find what works best for you and your goals. Be sure to give yourself space to take breaks, explore, and change things around throughout the writing process, without too much stress or rigidity. Remember, you will have the editing process to work things out any structural or copywriting errors.

Finetuning the Work Through Editing

Although it is possible to edit your book on your own, many self-publishers choose to hire an editor to obtain an outsider's perspective and receive insight on details they may have missed. If you decide to hire an editor, be sure to find one who is comfortable and skilled in your genre. Editors with specialized skillsets can provide invaluable perspective and edits to your writing. Ask yourself what you are looking for in the editor. Do you need an editor who specializes in dialogue? Perhaps you are looking for one to pick apart your structure and organization to ensure good flow. Or, perhaps you need an editor who is skilled in mood development. Either way, make sure you know your editor's strengths, specialties, and comfort level with the material before hiring them.

Making Use of the Editing Process for Your Career

When you begin the editing process, you must bear in mind that this is about much more than the book in front of you. What you learn throughout this process is what you will take with you into the rest of your writing career, and it will help you formulate your future works while learning what to implement and what to avoid. The editing process is your chance to grow by looking back on what you have written reflectively, applying feedback, and developing your writing craft.

If you choose to invest in an editor or editing team, you can consider it an investment in your learning and, ultimately, your future success in writing. Over time, you will see your style, voice, and general writing skill improve. Working with an editor is one of the most remarkable ways to see this transformation happen and may even lead you to create new editions of previous works.

Understanding the Stages of Editing

Before you begin the editing process, you need to know which type of editing you need. There are three stages of the editing process, which are vastly different from each other and all equally important. The first stage of editing is the structural or developmental stage. You determine the big picture of the story and determine if the organization flows well enough to represent that big picture. The following stage is the line editing stage, which is where you begin to narrow the scope, finetuning the language, and making as many smaller edits as possible. This is a stage for a lot of experiments with moving things around, adding new (but relevant) information, or removing parts of the book altogether.

The next part of stage two is copyediting, which involves acute attention to things like spelling, punctuation, grammar, and passive voice. The third stage of editing is the proofreading stage, where you will give the work a few final passes to pick up any errors that may have been overlooked. In many cases, it's a good idea to hire a different editor for each of the three stages so that you can take advantage of their unique skillsets and avoid the risk of them becoming burnt out.

Hiring Multiple Editors

Regardless of whether you or another editor is editing your writing or a combined effort, it is crucial to keep in mind the importance of the editing stages: structural editing, line and copyediting, and proofreading. Begin with big-picture editing passes and work your way down to the most specific details. Because all editors bring different skills and perspectives to the table, your best bet may be to hire a different editor to work with you on each editing process phase.

Making a Good First Impression Through Title

According to experts, the title you choose for your book is one of the key elements that determines publication success. The book's title is crucial to the book metadata and will compose the first impression readers have of the work you have done. The title is the way your book introduces itself to the world. Your title must address a problem the reader has and provide a clear solution(s). Readers should be able to read the title and feel confident about what this book can provide to them and how it can make their life better.

Titles with explicit promises of good results are proven to engage readers. As you create your title, ask yourself what problems your book can solve for the reader, what sort of desirable skill your book will provide, or how your personal testimony and knowledge could make someone else's life better. The title should pique your reader's interest to a point where they can't wait to read more. Seek to capture the imagination of your readers, making them ponder what they might find in this book and how it could change their life. What elements of what you have to say is most fascinating, captivating, or life-changing? What kinds of emotional response do you want your story to produce in the reader? Take your time to brainstorm ideas and test out several titles until you find what works best.

Maintaining Clarity

Your title should be simple, concise, and quickly generated to search engines to increase viewership and revenue. If you are producing a guidebook, you may use the words' how to' in the title to increase the number of hits your book will receive on the various search engines. The words you use should clearly express that you have what the potential reader needs, wants, or desires most in life. Your title should communicate what the book is about and what readers can expect to read about. Statistically, if the book is a guidebook, sales can be expected to go up if the title includes the words 'How to' by providing potential buyers with precisely what they need to know about the book.

Catching Reader Attention

The title of your book should use catchy and creative language that make it unforgettable. Your goal is to establish a sense of character in your book and attract the readers. This attraction method may take on the form of fun, lighthearted language, humor, alliterations, or cleverness. Regardless of which way you develop this title, you should make sure it will roll off the tongue nicely, entice readers, and stick in their minds after reading it. Your title should be appropriate to the genre you are writing in and should be considerate of the target audience.

However, a romance novel's title would use much dreamier and more formal language than a horror novel title. That said, you should aim to stand out from other books in the genre.

Keeping it Concise

When drafting your book's title, be sure not to use any more words than you need to convey the book's theme. The shorter the title, the more likely it will show up in search engines.

Additionally, the title of the book is what will stick with readers for generations upon generations. For titles to be as memorable as possible, they should not be difficult to say or type comfortably. You should strive for a title that is easy to say in interviews and easy for people to pass between one another when recommending your book. The book title should be engaging enough to leave people feeling excited and interested, no matter how many times they have heard it. Do not make the title any longer than it needs to be. You can always expand on your description of the book using subtitles.

Making Use of Subtitles

If you are writing a nonfiction title specifically, it is likely you will not have enough space in the title to express what readers should expect from your book fully. In this case, subtitles can be used to increase clarity. Subtitles should be just as compelling as the title itself and should further expand on the desirable outcome described in the title. You want your title to show readers how your book can address solutions for the pain points in their lives. The subtitle is the perfect place to expand on how this will happen.

Seeking Feedback from Your Target Audience

As you work through the process of title generation, it is important to seek feedback from your target audience. The target audience is the people you are writing to, and they are also most well-versed in other works within your genre. They can tell you what they are looking for when it comes to choosing their next book to read. The best way to do this in today's world is to join a writing group or create your own community via social media. You can utilize tools like a Facebook writing group or a social media poll for the target audience to vote from a series of title options and provide further feedback.

Using Title Generation Tools

If you feel stuck on how to generate your title, there is no need to worry. There are endless options for title generators that can help get you started. Book title generators take what you want your title to express and apply a wide selection of names and formats to choose from. However, it is crucial to be aware of titles that fall flat. In many cases, the titles you generate on a tool should be used more as a source of inspiration than the book's actual title.

Chapter 3: Step 3 - Intermediate Stages

As a self-publisher, your job is to publish your media in the most creative and engaging way possible. The front cover of a book is especially crucial to design. After the title, your cover is the first thing a reader can look at to consider whether or not they will begin to read the book. In this sense, cover design serves a significant purpose in communicating the message of the book. The book cover should include the author's name, the title, and any other elements or images that will intrigue the reader. The book's spine should have the title and author's name for easy identification, and the back cover should list the ISBN, author biography, and any good reader testimonies.

Making Use of the Elements of Book Design

The first element of book design is the front matter, which is all of the information readers will see first. This includes title pages, copyright pages, the table of contents, and forewords, prefaces, and introductions when needed. The second element is the book's body matter, which comprises the book chapters and sections. The third and final element is the back matter, which is the last parts of the book, including epilogues, appendices, and author biographies.

Laying out Interior Book Design

When it comes to laying out the book's interior, you have a lot of layout elements and formats at your disposal.

If you aren't sure which layout format to choose, try examining several of the books on your own bookshelf to find the fonts, layout, and trim size you like best. If you're not sure where to start, consider the following tips:

· Select a legible font and use at least 11 pt. size or larger

· Use 1.5 line spacing for easy legibility that does not use too much or too little space between sentences

· Number the pages of the book for clarity purposes

· Start chapters on the right-hand side of the page

Designing Your Book Cover

As previously mentioned, the front cover is an incredibly crucial element of book design. As you design your book cover or work with a designer who does, make sure to use visually appealing graphics. The cover should use imagery that elicits an emotional response and clearly communicates to the reader what they can expect. Any photos or graphics you use on the front cover should be in high resolution (you can find such images on stock photo sites, many of which are free).

Before diving into cover design, it is a good idea to explore other books' covers in your genre. What style of graphics and font are used for the title and the author's name? What elements are placed on the cover and spine, and what is their general placement? How do the graphic elements of the cover interact with the text? What can the reader glen from the book cover concerning the theme of the book? As you study the books on your own bookshelf, you can better understand the ways book covers should be designed to create a connection with the reader, inflict emotional responses, and lead them to read your book.

Choosing a Professional Designer

Just as it is useful to invest in editors for your self-published book, it is beneficial to invest in designers. People are naturally drawn to images, and the more visually engaging your book is, the more likely readers will be to pick it up. Professional designers are trained to take a topic at hand and represent it in a visually engaging way, and they can often see things that you as the writer cannot. This is why it can be smart to invest in someone who does design for a living. Remember, there are several facets of book design. The first of these is print design, the second is ebook design, and the third is a website and digital media design. Just as it can be beneficial to invest in outside editors for your book, it can help you invest in designers.

In most cases, you cannot expect a single designer to specialize in print, ebook, and Website/digital media design, which may warrant the use of multiple designers. Before hiring a design professional, make sure you have all of the editing finished. After that piece is finished, you can often contact your local Chamber of Commerce or utilize social media to reach out to graphic designers in your area. If you want to hire a professional, there are several things to consider.

First, you should ask any candidates to provide you with a portfolio to examine the style and quality of the work they do and if they have experience with book design. Next, you will need to ask them for a price quote for design work so you can actively plan for that in your budget. After that, you will need to ask them how they handle revision requests and what general process they follow. Finally, you will need to clarify your ownership of the artwork. Feel free to ask for samples of books they have designed for other clients and clarify which program they will be using to do the design work.

Striking a Balance in Description

After the title and the book cover, your book description is likely the next place the reader will go to decide if they are interested in your book. The description leads readers to determine whether this book is worth their time, money, and energy. The description should include just enough information about what happens in the book to captivate the reader and make them hungry to read on. You have to strike a balance between revealing the plot's basis without providing too many details or giving away the ending. The reader should understand the basic setting and context of the story from your description, but they should not know the entire storyline.

When designing the hook sentence of your book description, you need to ask yourself what major issue is at hand in this book. What is the problem you need to solve? Use your creativity to create an engaging sentence that describes the problem that needs to be solved and makes it personal to the reader. Don't shy away from emotion in writing your description—play into it. Play into the main character's fears, suffering, or joys to spark empathy and give the reader a taste of the emotional experience they can expect in this book.

Maintaining Third Person Point of View

Another major thing to keep in mind in writing your book description is writing in the third person point of view. When writing a book description, you should avoid talking too much about yourself. If you do refer to yourself, for example, in a brief author byline, be sure to refer to yourself by your pronouns (he/she/they/ etc.) to maintain the third person point of view. If you include an author byline, be sure it is separated from the rest of the book as a short paragraph after the teaser for the book itself.

Using Testimonials and Endorsements

At the end of your book description, you should use testimonials or endorsements (as long as they enhance the description itself). Testimonials should come from someone who has read the book and had a satisfying experience or found the solution to their reading problem. You can reach out to your fanbase to submit testimonials, and even offer incentives for the best ones.

An endorsement typically comes from an authority figure who your readers are likely to recognize who has read the book and agrees that the content is beneficial, and you are qualified as an author. In many cases, celebrities, popular media sources, or other authors in the genre can be used to provide endorsements.

Practicing Description Writing

The last tip for writing book descriptions is to practice. Draw inspiration from the techniques used by other writers in your genre. Try highlighting different details, using different language, and experimenting with various hooks and conclusions to the description. Make a file on your computer dedicated only to the descriptions of a particular book, and feel free to share it with your network. Remember, it is normal and necessary to have multiple drafts of the same book description.

Revise it as many times as you need to feel like it perfectly describes your book. It is always a good idea to seek feedback from colleagues, mentors, or potential readers to offer their perspective. After they have looked over the description, you can ask them a series of questions to determine whether or not they truly got the message. Based on what they just read, what do they expect the book to be about? What excites them going forward? What areas are still unclear? Do they feel interested in reading on? If not, what could be changed that would pique their interest? Listen carefully to other views, as their suggestions speak to the more considerable reader experience and readers' likelihood to buy your book.

Chapter 4: Step 4 - Costs to Keep in Mind

One of the most critical steps of the self-publishing process is establishing a budget that includes all the costs and that you can stick to. The budget is ultimately up to you; some authors release ebooks as inexpensive as $1,000-$3,000, while other authors may spend much more. Regardless of where you fall on this spectrum, you must understand that all costs associated with publishing the book are your responsibility.

Within this budget, you need to think of people you may need to hire, such as professional editors and designers, as well as technical things like an ISBN, cover photos, copyright, typesetting, your own website, distribution tactics, various advertising and marketing strategies, and other miscellaneous costs. Before you begin your budgeting process, ask yourself how much money you are willing to spend and how well you want your book to sell. While it is possible to self-publish a book on a tight budget, you need to make sure you're not skimping on any details. If you let too many things slip through the cracks for the purpose of saving money, your book will be of lower quality and, therefore, less likely to sell well.

Investing in the Editing Process

Perhaps one of the most essential areas to budget for is the investment in a professional editor. Although it is possible to edit your book on your own, you can create a more polished version of your text if you hire a professional editor (or several) to look over your book and catch any issues with flow, context, spelling, punctuation, grammar, or general content. Even if you are a successful editor yourself, having another pair of eyes to copyedit, proofread, and check your work for consistency can make all the difference in the world.

Because the editing process has multiple stages, you may want to consider budgeting enough to pay editors who specialize in each step. In many cases, the editing stages take up the most considerable portion of costs for self-publishing. Professional editing can cost anywhere between $300-$1,500 on average. If all you need is line editing on a short book, you will probably not have to spend more than $150-$300. However, if you are in need of developmental or structural editing, you should expect to pay much more than that, depending on the length of the book. Additionally, if you choose to hire a ghostwriter, you should plan to spend more.

Investing in Cover Design

Another vital investment to make is in the book's cover design. In some cases, authors are talented in design and choose to design their own covers to make the project even more their own. This can be great for writers who also have particular skillsets in design, but if you are questioning your design skills at all, it's best to either hire someone or invest in a program to help you. If you want to play a part in your own cover design but don't know where to get started, you can access templates and other services on things like Amazon's Cover Creator or licensed images or templates from Canva.

If you are on a tight budget, you can access stock photography options for your cover photo (and any other images throughout the book). If you have a bit more money to dedicate to the cover, you may consider investing in a professional photo shoot to obtain your cover photo. You should also consider whether or not you want a professional headshot on your book cover, as this is an extra cost. Professional cover design typically costs between $100-$600. There are several less expensive options, such as designers who are just starting out and hoping to gain exposure or work that has already been created that you are merely paying to reuse. That said, it is vital to make sure you're not skimping on the cover design. As discussed earlier in the book, the cover is the first impression readers will receive of your book, and it is worth an investment.

Investing in Interior Design

You also need to keep in mind the costs of your books' interior design. This is especially important if you are planning to release a print copy of the book, in which case you should plan to have your text professionally typeset. Typesetting is complex and requires a lot of skill, time, and energy, and you should prepare to make this investment in any print book. If you are releasing an eBook and are searching for customization beyond what you can find on Amazon's Kindle Create, ePub, or similar platforms, you may wish to hire a designer to help.

If you have a larger budget, you may also consider investing in a graphic designer for things like book posters, bookmarks, and business cards. It is a good idea to include general formatting costs in your design costs, ranging from $50-$300. If you're on a tight budget, you may consider looking into free or inexpensive online options for editing book interiors—just be cautious.

If you plan to sell print copies of your book, you should invest in print proofs to double-check the layouts and catch any final errors. IngramSpark can be used for paperback books, and it typically costs $30 per print proof. If you have a team of designers and editors, you will need to invest in a proof copy for each person. If you are printing your book, keep in mind that there will be fees charged by the printers.

Investing in Online Advertisements and Websites

While it is optional, many authors choose to invest in advertisements on social media, magazines, or TV to increase publicity and sales. Some companies assist with marketing and media exposure for a fee. In many cases, authors choose to create a website in which to promote themselves and build a community among their target audience. Your website can serve as an author platform through which to write blogs, expand your business, and gain publicity for your works.

Whether you choose a paid website developer or choose to use a free one like WordPress or Blogger, there are several costs you should be prepared to be responsible for. The first of these is website hosting, which generally costs around $150 per year. You may also need to purchase a domain name, especially if you want to increase the number of people who find your website. The cost for a domain name is relatively low, at around $10-$15 annually.

Lastly, if you want to collect email addresses to compile a mailing list, you will need to pay for an email subscription service. This service will manage all of your emails. In many cases, you can find an email subscription service for as low as $10 per month, depending on how many subscribers you have. If you are hoping to run ads on your website, you should set aside a budget of between $100-$500.

Making Technical Investments

In terms of more technical self-publishing investments, you should be prepared to invest in an ISBN. The ISBN is a unique code that will allow bookstores and libraries to access the book's necessary information quickly. While there are free options that exist (such as CreateSpace and IngramSpark), your book is less likely to be carried in bookstores if you don't invest any money in it. Free ISBNs cause further limitations in that they prohibit eBooks from being stocked on Overdrive, which is a website that circulates eBooks to public libraries worldwide. The cost of getting an ISBN is $295 for 10 ISBN codes, which is worth it when you consider all of the channels of distribution it will open up for you.

Determining Miscellaneous Budget Items

There are several final miscellaneous items to include in your budget. The first of these is the cost to register your manuscript with the Library of Congress and get it copyrighted. You should plan for events such as book signings or release parties and the costs associated with those. Additionally, you should save room in your budget for random logistical items such as shipping, packaging, office supplies, and bookstands. You may also choose to have your book made into an audiobook, which is generally an added cost of between $300-$3,000 (again depending on the length of the book). It is a good idea to have a specific portion of your budget set aside for the miscellaneous items, so you can be prepared to foot unexpected costs if they arise

Budget Planning in Three Categories

As you begin to plan your budget, it's best to divide the process into three categories. First, you should determine what you can comfortably accomplish yourself (while making sure they are still professional and that you can be free of errors). Second, you should evaluate the things you need to pay someone else to do and where you plan to look for those people to hire. Lastly, ask yourself what items you may be able to barter for with friends.

If you have a friend who is a graphic designer, for example, they may be able to help you with your cover or interior design for a discounted price. If you have a friend who works as an editor, you may be able to share your skills with them in exchange for them to do an editing pass on your book. No matter how you choose to divide the three categories in your budgeting process, you need to make sure you have generated an all-encompassing total cost. Once you have determined this total cost, you can determine how many copies of your book you'll need to sell to break even and how many you would need to sell to profit.

Chapter 5: Step 5 - Marketing and Distribution

When it comes to self-publishing, marketing is one of the greatest keys to success. Before you even begin to write your book, you should begin marketing. You should be able to identify the *why*, that is, the reason you are choosing to write this book. You should then identify the *what*, which describes what impact you hope the book will have and what your readers have to gain from it. As previously described, you should be sure to determine who your market is, what they want, and how your book can satisfy that need and create the impact you desire. Once you have answered these key questions, you will have a greater sense of direction in your marketing strategy.

Developing your Marketing Campaign

When you approach the book marketing process, you should do so as you would approach any other businesses. Marketing campaigns take a great deal of skill and attention to detail to accurately portray your audience's gain from your book. How can you help the people who will read your book? How will their life be better after reading it? Once you have answered these questions, you will have a direction for communicating with your readers and making it clear to them why they should read your book.

Investing in Communication

As a self-publisher, you should invest in communication with your readers. This communication can take on many forms. Some self-publishers choose to spend hours researching within their niche and reading others' work, so they know the best and most current tips and tricks to use. Other self-publishers invest time in learning strategies of online traffic keywords to direct more attention to their works. Some spend a great deal of time investing in their social media and generating a following through which to gain readers. Some may opt for a more traditional method of placing their book in physical spaces, such as libraries, bookstores, or other stores and having tables at conventions and other events.

Marketing Using Book Reviews

In many cases, you can use book reviews as a way to market your book. Book reviews use persuasive language and are editorial, not promotional, which makes them appear more genuine. Honest reviews of your book help it be seen for what it is and make it clear to your audience what they are getting into. You can also use author platforms, such as a personal website and your social media accounts. In today's world, online marketing is often more effective and less expensive than traditional strategies.

Implementing a Planning Process

One of the most critical aspects of marketing is the planning process. The most effective planning process has several, which are as follows: segment your markets, target your best customers, understand how, when, and where your customers buy books, and what motivates them to do so, and create a position through which to bring in targeted customers.

Determining Top Markets

When it comes to segmenting your customers, you must remember that it is impossible to check every reader's box. It is essential to understand how different people may choose to use your book and those who are most likely to make frequent investments for their purposes.

You will likely come up with a long list of potential buyers, and you should know that it is impossible to market to all of them equally. From the list, you should come up with your top markets, which will create your targets. Developing your target groups does not mean you are ignoring individuals who are not in those groups; it merely means they are not your focus.

Marketing to the Needs of the Target Audience

As your buyers decide which books to buy, they have a number of things they are looking for. If you are writing a book that targets college-aged voters, you may find that your book would do best in an election year, as tensions are high, and voting is a topic of higher focus. Your target audience may be motivated to buy your book if they know it can tell them what they need to know to form their opinions on voting and have their questions answered.

Your position, then, would be the way you use the topic that motivates your target audience. In this case, you may adopt a position of addressing the fact that college-aged voters may feel intimidated by voting and have questions they are afraid to ask. You can approach them from a place of non-judgment that will help them get all the answers they need to be informed voters in the upcoming election.

Understanding the Buying Process

When it comes to marketing, you should also understand the stages of the buying process. The buying process has five steps: problem recognition, informative search, alternative evaluation, purchase decision, and post-purchase evaluation. Understanding this model is crucial if you want to sell your book.

Problem Recognition

The first step of the process, problem recognition, happens when a buyer realizes they have a problem. In your college-aged voter target audience, the problem is that they feel intimidated about voting and are full of questions they don't know how to get answered. In order to sell your book to them, you must prove why the information within it provides a solution to this problem by answering their questions and equipping them with useful information about voting, so they feel more confident.

You must be aware of the fact that problems vary greatly depending on the market you are working within and the population of your target audience. Nonfiction books, like the one about voting, are geared towards educating the reader and being informative to obtain the desired solution. Fiction books, however, are more focused on solving entertainment-related problems.

Evaluating Alternatives

Once a buyer has discovered they have a problem, they will start looking for a way to solve that problem. This leads to the second stage of the process, which is evaluating alternatives. In this stage, the buyer is thinking of various ways to solve their problem, and they likely will be trying to choose between several books to get the solutions. In this case, it can be helpful to provide free samples of your writing that will give the reader a taste and further implore them to purchase your book.

Making the Right Choice

After they have evaluated alternatives, they will move into a phase of deciding whether or not to make the purchase. At this point, the buyer will be worried about making the right choice. This is an opportunity to follow up with them and encourage them towards the purchase by explaining how it will be worth it and improving their lives. It is imperative not to lose connection with potential buyers during this stage. Overall, you must have a good understanding of your customer's buying processes to plan out your timing.

Adhering to the Buyer's Timeline

Be prepared that customers will all function at slightly different timings, and you should seek to adhere to their schedules. That said, you should be ready to intercept multiple customers at multiple times and in numerous contexts. You may use your website or social media accounts to have giveaways, question and answer sessions, or teasers to keep your readers engaged and promote your work.

Mastering Online Distribution

Equally important to marketing your book in the world, is distributing it. From the time you begin to tell potential buyers about your book, you should be thinking of the most effective ways to get it into their hands. In today's world of technology, you should know that more than half of all book sales (both print and eBooks) take place online. This is crucial knowledge for the self-publisher when it comes to distribution, and it can be used to your advantage in that you have the same, inexpensive access to the online world as any major publishers do. When it comes to book retailers, Amazon is ranked highest globally, no matter the format of the books being sold.

One way to get your book circling online is by creating direct relationships with online retailers. If you are in communication with these online retailers, you will have more control and access to marketing and promotion tools. If you work with eBook distribution services, you will likely have to give up a certain percentage of your profits. However, many of these distributors have access to exclusive promotion and marketing tools, which may help you reach a wider audience and sell more copies.

Determining Print Distribution Options

In terms of distributing print books, print-on-demand options are typically best for new self-publishers. Print-on-demand means that your book will not be printed until after someone has ordered and paid for it. Each order constitutes one printed book, which will then be shipped out to the paying customer. Printing on demand reduces the risk of spending too much money on printing and having many books leftover. That said, it also reduces the likelihood that your book will be sitting on the shelves of popular retailers. It is essential to look at your budget and weigh out the pros and cons when deciding how to distribute your print book.

Making Use of Aggregators

Whether you are planning to distribute digitally or in print, you will want to know how to use an aggregator. Aggregators are companies that allow you to upload your books to a single place, from which they will be distributed to other platforms. Several popular aggregators are Smashwords, IngramSpark, PublishDrive, and Draft2Digital.Out of these, IngramSpark is the one that allows for single uploads for both eBook and print. Most other aggregators require separate uploads to be made. You can use a variety of distributors in combination with other another or separately.

There is no set answer for how many aggregators to make use of at one time. If you have the time and energy, it's a good idea to spread yourself across various individual platforms. When you do this, your royalties will go up, and you may have increased access to things like promotions.

Choosing a Distributor

When it comes to what to look for in a distributor, there are several factors to consider. The first thing you should do is compare the reputations of various distributors. What are other authors saying about this distributor? If the reviews you find are mostly negative or have trouble locating reviews in general, it's best to steer clear. To that same token, you must take into account the reliability of the distributor. Is their service known for reliable content delivery to readers? After you have determined this, you should assess the ease of use of a particular distributor. You want the service(s) you choose to be as quick and painless as possible in terms of digital file publishing and distribution. Lastly, you should examine your budget and compare the cost-effectiveness of various distributors. Make sure to look at every detail of cost involved so you can identify the actual price and compare which distributors are the best value for the money.

Chapter 6: Step 6 - Self-Publishing Mistakes to Avoid

Like in every industry, there are numerous mistakes in the self-publishing field that you should be aware of and take action to avoid. The self-publishing industry is becoming more extensive and more competitive by the day, and therefore, it is more important than ever to be diligent in preventing mistakes.

Being Lazy with Editing

One of the first significant mistakes you can make in self-publishing is to be lazy with the editing process. Grammar and spelling errors, inconsistencies, and clichés may seem insignificant at times, but in reality, these things pose massive stumbling blocks to the reader. Books that are poorly edited are challenging to get through and do not gain the same respect in the industry as their well-edited counterparts.

While there are self-publishers who edit their own work, you have to be meticulous and conduct far more editing passes (with sufficient breaks in between) than you may think necessary. Better still is to edit the book a time or two yourself, then hire a professional editor or editing team for each of the types of editing. Before sending your book out into the world, you must make sure that it has undergone enough editing passes to have every stage of the process completed.

Formatting Incorrectly

Along the same lines as editing, another fatal flaw of a self-publisher is incorrectly formatting the book. It is crucial to make yourself aware of the various stipulations booksellers have in place and abide by those standards in your formatting process. Be sure to thoroughly read the guidelines and note the required file types, graphic formatting, and general manuscript formatting requirements (such as line spacing, paragraphs, and section breaks).

Failing to Reach Out

Not only do some authors fail to have proper editing and formatting, but they also fail to open up the book to trusted members of the target audience to provide feedback. If no one reads your book before it is published, you will send it out into the world with no idea of what your readers will enjoy or the places it still needs work. Friends, family members, and trusted audience members can provide honest feedback and shed light on areas you may not have previously noticed. Better yet is to join a writing community that provides both support and necessary criticism. Not being willing to accept criticism is one major flaw of many self-publishers, and it can truly impact the overall success of that book.

Slacking on Cover Design

Another major self-publishing mistake is making the minimal effort on your cover design. As mentioned previously, the cover of your book is the first impression—it sets a precedent for the rest of the book and helps readers decide whether they are initially interested or not. In an attempt to save money, many authors choose to create their own front covers with minimal design experience. The authors who do this probably assume that the rest of their book will be enough to capture the reader's attention, and therefore, that it's okay to have an average cover.

The problem with this is that if the cover is unappealing, the reader will not even bother to look over other book elements. If you can't hook them with the cover, you have almost no hope of getting them to the next step of the decision process; they will simply rule out your book without a second thought. Therefore, unless you are skilled in design and publishing techniques, the decision to skimp on the cover of your book could completely tank your sales.

Writing a Poor Book Description

Earlier in the chapter, we discussed the importance of a good book description. After the cover, your book description is the next impression of the book as a whole, and you have to make it count. A crucial mistake many self-publishers make is to be boring, rambling, or self-righteous in their description. If readers feel disengaged, lost, or condescended, it is an immediate turn-off from reading the rest of the book. To avoid making this mistake, you should make an effort to read as many example descriptions from your genre as possible. What are the typical structures authors use? What plot points are highlighted? The more familiar you are with these strategies, the more likely you are to engage your reader and set a helpful precedent for the rest of the book.

Losing Sight of the Market

Another common mistake self-publishers make is not taking the time to analyze the market. The best self-publishers know what types of books are selling and why, and they know how to play into those statistics. Not taking the time to conduct thorough research on the market, potential competition, and your demographic can be a crucial mistake. To that same token, not marketing at all is another fatal flaw of many self-publishers. If people haven't heard of their book, they will have no reason to buy it.

As a self-publisher, you must be able to talk about yourself and the work that you do, even before it is published. In a world of ever-growing technology, you will not be able to reach your full potential unless you fully take advantage of marketing via social media. Use things like polls, questions and answers, and teasers to keep your readers and fans engaged with the writing process from start to finish, ultimately giving them no choice but to buy the book when it is released. Identify your personal network of friends, family, followers, and your writing community, rely on them to help you with promotion and buy their book for themselves or gift to other people in their lives. Do not be afraid to ask your support system to promote you.

Releasing Books at the Wrong Time

When it comes to releasing books into the world, timing is crucial. Lousy timing can destroy your book's potential for success completely. Pay attention to the calendar. What season are you releasing your book in? How do members of your audience often react to that season? What is the political and cultural climate? What are the significant events of the day? What are people talking about? All of these are crucial considerations when it comes to the timing of releasing your book. How can the release of your book correspond with what is happening in the world?

Losing Track of Your Release Date

Another major mistake self-publishers make is failing to select and stick to a particular release date in terms of timing. Throughout the marketing process, you must be able to cultivate audience expectations and set the tone of yourself as a reliable person. When arranging your release date, be realistic. Don't push yourself to deadlines you may not be able to reach—give yourself more time than you need to leave room for things to go wrong. If you give yourself this leeway, you can avoid letting your audience down.

Selling your Book for the Wrong Price

When you go to sell your book, another major mistake to look out for is trying to sell it for the wrong price. If the price is too high, people will not only not buy your book but also respect it less. If it is too low, your sales may increase, but you will not be profiting in the way you deserve. Additionally, if a book is priced too low, readers may draw conclusions about the book's quality and assume that it's too cheap to be worth the read. The best way to avoid mispricing your book is to research other books' average prices within your genre. Additionally, it's a good idea to analyze how other authors use promotional discounts and be smart with your personal use to increase your sales.

Limiting Distribution Channels

In an earlier chapter, we discussed the variety of channels through which to distribute your book. While it can be possible to achieve success using only one distributor, this can also be a mistake. In many cases, self-publishers restrict themselves and the book's potential success by using only one channel. To avoid this, allow yourself to use as many distributors as physically possible. What do you have to lose?

Losing Faith in the Face of Failure

The final major mistake self-publishers make to quit if the first book doesn't do well. This is a cutthroat industry, and persistence is absolutely crucial if you want to "make it" as an author. To keep your spirits up, you should view each book you write as an experience from which to grow, no matter the outcome. Each failure is fuel for future success, and you must be patient and persistent. The worst mistake you can make is to give up too soon. Don't rush yourself—take all the necessary actions and then allow things to happen in their time. By doing things right the first time, you can increase your chances for success once the book is out in the world.

When you have finished writing your first book, allow yourself to celebrate what you have accomplished. Writing a book is a massive accomplishment in itself, and one you should be proud of yourself for achieving. With every book you write, you have the chance to develop your fan base, change your strategy, and continue to increase your popularity. Although this chapter has been focused on the mistakes to avoid, it is also important to remember that mistakes are part of the growth process. With each book you write and mistake you commit; you have a chance to try something new the next time.

Chapter 7: Step 7 - Tips for Successful Self-Publishers

In the previous chapter, we discussed the significant mistakes for self-publishers to avoid. This chapter will seek to engage in reframing mistakes to avoid into secrets to apply to your writing process. Throughout this chapter, we will discuss several tips to unlock your most profound potential as a self-publisher, and truly set yourself apart from others.

Taking it Step by Step

The first tip for successful self-publishers goes hand in hand with the mistakes to avoid. As previously mentioned, cutting corners in editing, design, or marketing can abolish a book's potential for success. If your book is sloppily edited, you will lose reader's attention, respect, and level of enjoyment in reading. If you slack on design, your book will be easily overlooked on the shelves, and readers will be discouraged from taking even the first step in engaging with your text. If you are closeminded in your marketing strategies, or worse yet, don't engage in marketing at all, you will have done all of that work only to sell very few copies.

Ultimately, if you choose to go on the journey of self-publishing, go there fully, without cutting corners. By choosing to be thorough in every single part of the process, checking, double-checking, and reaching out for professional help and outsider perspective, your book has the potential to go from good to extraordinary. While it is important to keep costs in mind, you will need to be careful not to sell yourself short. When you set out to self-publish a book, you should set out with the decision to invest in the parts of the process that will enhance your level of success.

Finding Your Niche

The next tip is to be acutely aware of your niche and what kind of content you want to write within that niche. Every human being has particular gifts and passions and a unique life story and way of seeing the world. Perhaps you are a naturally sensitive, hopeless romantic who sees the beauty in nearly every person and place you encounter. Knowing this about yourself, you would likely determine that the place for you is within the niche of romance novel writing. After you have determined that, ask yourself what parts of your perception on romance could make for an interesting story. Locate the gaps that exist in the niche, and ask yourself how you can fill them.

After you have taken time to analyze all of your contributions, passions, interest areas, and experiences, narrow it down to the niche where you have the most to say and will be most well-received. Be sure to keep the context in mind—what element of your story or perspective is most applicable to your target audience? What is the target audience most in need of from your content? Why does the world need this book, and what qualifies you to be the one to write it? Once you have answered these questions, you can effectively narrow down your options to identify your content's best potential niche(s). You can use your target audience's needs to guide your writing process and marketing strategies and cultivate your fanbase and potential for future successes.

Establishing Realistic Goals

Before you begin writing, you should be aware of your personal goals. Why have you decided to set out on this journey? Knowing your purpose and what you hope to provide and gain through the self-publishing experience can more accurately shape your process. Having a clear picture in your head allows you to set realistic goals for your needs and what you hope to achieve. Let's say that one of your goals is to sell a high number of books. You must look at your experience and define "a lot of books" accordingly.

If you are new at self-publishing and have not yet had the chance to establish an audience, you should start a relatively low number and work your way up. Establish a plan for how to expand your author platform, build a fanbase, and market yourself so that your sales can regularly progress. Take time to develop a thorough business plan with daily action steps. What will you do every day to remain consistent with your goals? Take several sticky notes and write your goals on them, then paste them all over your workspace so you can constantly remind yourself the reason for starting this journey, and motivate yourself to stay on it.

Relationship Building and Collaboration

Earlier in the book, we discussed the importance of building your team and trading off skills with friends, professionals, fans, and a writing community. Collaborative relationships open the doors for you to try new things, gain new perspectives and chances for exposure, and cultivate new strategies for success. It is crucial to know who your network is and tap into that. How can your story grow stronger by playing off the insight of your community? Where is your target audience showing up, and how can you meet them there?

In addition to the relationships mentioned, it is also useful to collaborate with outside organizations, non-profits, and community events. You can collaborate with schools, libraries, local bookstores, etc. for book tours, signings, and other events to boost your exposure. You should dedicate plenty of time to researching what's happening with your community, and drafting pitches to various organizations about why the promotion of your book can benefit their organization.

Always Keep Writing

The final tip for self-publishing success is to keep writing, even if you're hitting a wall or feel like the book is finished. Don't let your writing go stagnant—challenge yourself to write a little bit every day, implementing different prompts and techniques. You can keep up with writing by using daily journals, writing entries on your author blog, writing monthly newspaper or magazine columns, or simply sitting down with a pen and paper for a brainstorming session. By continuing to write, you can develop your professional skills and continue to get the word out about the books you've written and the role you play as an author in your niche. Continue to add to your portfolio, book as many events as possible, and remain in a constant state of seeking new opportunities to grow your author platform.

Making a Daily Commitment

When you choose to embark on the self-publishing journey, you must understand that you are making a daily commitment. As a self-published author, you must commit to waking up every day with something new to learn, plan, or complete. You must create a life around who you are as an author and learn to find opportunities for success in every corner of the world. You should view the world as your toolbox, taking inspiration from the people and events around you, as well as the passions, skills, and interests you have been gifted with.

Conclusion

You picked up this guide with the understanding that the self-publishing route was the route you wanted to go and the desire to dive into the logistics of the journey. You likely began this guide with an understanding of the industry's cutthroat nature and the preparedness to learn the details of every part of the process. You understood that in order to be successful, you had to familiarize yourself with the mistakes other self-publishers have made, as well as their secrets to rising to the top of the industry. You had an awareness of all that is at stake in the self-publishing process, especially as it pertains to setting yourself apart from other writers within your genre.

At the start of this guide, you were introduced to the things that set self-publishing apart from publishing with a company. You learned that you have more agency through self-publishing and can call all the shots on marketing, design, and showcasing your creativity. You are in charge of every element of your book, from the beginning of the process to the end, and you can operate freely from publishing companies. When you become a successful self-publisher, there is truly nothing that can stand in your way on your journey to the top.

Throughout the guide, you were provided with the ins and outs of the self-publishing process, from the beginning stages of writing, editing, and generating a title, to the intermediate stages of book design and description writing, to the details of budgeting, marketing, and distribution. You learned the importance of reaching out to other people on a personal and professional level to guide you and make sure you are staying on track with your intentions and appeals to the target audience.

You learned what mistakes to avoid to be as successful as possible, as well as the secret tips of the most successful self-publishers. You learned how to establish yourself as a reliable and well-respected author who regularly engages with their fanbase and keeps the fans involved in the process. You learned how to make your own process and use your creativity, voice, and marketing strategies to your advantage, as well as tips for how and where to distribute.

You discovered the importance of being thorough throughout every step of the process, as well as the benefits of reaching out for help from professional editors and designers. You learned the importance hearing from the target audience members to ask for advice and perspective. You learned that in order to distinguish yourself as a self-published author, you must identify the gaps that exist in your genre and decide how you can fill them. You also discovered the benefits of breaking each stage down into a multi-step process to keep yourself and your team on track.

Throughout the course of this guide, you have learned every skill you need to become a successful self-publisher. With this guide by your side as your trusty self-publishing guide, nothing can steer you wrong!

Book 3: How to Write Sales Copy

7 Easy Steps to Master Copywriting, Marketing Content, Business Writing & Freelance Writing

Jaiden Pemton

Introduction

In a world that is brimming with products to be sold, and thousands of avenues through which to sell them, you have to create a truly convincing sales copy in order to be successful. In order to do this, you must have an understanding not only of the market you are writing into, but also, the particular language and strategies to use when appealing to that market. When it comes to advertising, it is crucial to meet people, recognize their struggles and what they want, and show them how your product or service can benefit them in the quickest and most clear-cut way possible.

This guide will show you exactly how to do these things, which will set you apart in sales copywriting and gain you more sales than your competitors.

The sales world is complicated because most people have much more pressing issues in their life than which products and services to buy. Not only that, but every niche is full of hundreds, if not thousands of options for products and services. With social media especially, the sky is truly the limit in terms of advertising. The task of making your product or service stand out can be incredibly daunting, especially when it comes to keeping the reader's attention and making them care. The industry leaves no room for error, and therefore it is crucial to develop skills that set you apart and help you achieve the necessary number of sales.

When it comes to sales copywriting, it is easy to fall into the trap of presenting your product or service from your perspective instead of your reader's perspective. You may struggle to determine how to organize your sales copy, how to appeal to the audience of a particular niche, or how to create a lasting and sustainable impact. Another common challenge is developing credibility, which will reassure your readers enough to invest. In many cases, sales copies do not check all the boxes to answer audience questions and address concerns. Often, the content is dry, and the significant points become lost in the text, with the readers' attention-getting lost right alongside it. Luckily, this guide has everything you need in a comprehensive step-by-step reference format to become an expert sales copywriter.

This guide will provide you with the in-depth knowledge you need to determine your audience, develop a compelling sales page, tell meaningful stories, rebut the neigh sayers, appeal to emotion, and call your readers to the desired action. Additionally, the guide contains top secret tips to distinguishing yourself as a sales copywriter and avoiding the common mistakes writers make within this genre.

The chapters of this guide will take you through each step of the sales copywriting process to avoid common mistakes and develop your thorough strategy. Each chapter is designed with astounding detail to help you stay on track and address any questions or concerns you have along the way.

Chapters are subtitled and easy-to-follow with examples of tips, tricks, techniques, and things to avoid. No matter what you are aiming to advertise through your sales copies or who your audience is, this guide has all the tools you need and is sure to serve as the perfect guide to revolutionize your sales copywriting experience.

Happy writing!

Chapter 1: Step 1 - Determining your Sale Copy Audience

When it comes to writing a sales copy, discovering your target audience is perhaps the most critical piece of the puzzle. This process is one to which you should dedicate a lot of time and energy, allowing yourself to be thorough and intentional with the questions you ask and the steps you take to understand your audience better. It is best to begin by asking yourself several questions to understand your product's goals fully. Why does your product exist in the first place, and what problems does it work to solve?

Defining Product Purpose

If you are writing about a natural all-purpose cleaner, for example, the product exists to provide consumers with an effective everyday housecleaning method without harmful chemicals and toxins. This product was developed to solve customers' problems of potentially becoming ill from toxic chemicals in their household cleaners and needing to find an alternative option. Your sales copy, therefore, should appeal to audience members who are trying to solve this problem. By defining your product purpose, you can better understand why your content exists and is worth people's time and money, who will take the time to read about your product, and what they value most. You should also be aware of your competition within the industry.

What other products are on the market that resemble your product, and what sets your product apart from the others? You must provide customers with a clear idea of what they gain from choosing your work instead of a competitor's; one of the best ways to do this is by demonstrating what you do better than anyone else.

In the case of writing a sales copy about an all-purpose cleaner, you should assume that your audience consists of people who own homes and are in the socioeconomic position to care about keeping them clean. Additionally, you are likely appealing to adults who are educated in matters of health and the environment, and want to make the best choices for themselves and their family.

This audience is aware of the harm cleaning products can cause to the environment and the body, and it is your job to provide them with further statistics and proof of why your product is the best. You would need to be careful not to assume too much, however, because you very likely have people who want to protect their health and environment but are new to the concept of natural cleaning products. Therefore, you must master the correct way to address both people who are aware of the benefits of natural cleaning products, and those who are still exploring.

Elements of Audience Definition

After these initial considerations of product purpose, customer goals and values, and what sets your product apart from competitors, you are ready to create your audience definition. The three elements to an audience definition are the product or service being advertised, the content's mission, and the primary audience demographic. In the case of the household cleaner, your audience definition may look something like this.

"ShiningDay All-Purpose Cleaner exists to provide effective, all-natural alternatives to daily household cleaners for *anyone* who maintains a living space and cares about their health, so they can avoid the detrimental long-term health effects of chemicals in most household cleaning products."

Addressing Audience Struggles

As you develop your audience definition, be sure to place most of your emphasis on what your audience is struggling with (instead of the shallow demographics of who they are). It is easy to assume that an audience who maintains a living space and values their health may struggle with knowing which products to buy to work for their purposes and protect their health. Your appeal to the audience should develop under these terms of what they are struggling with and how your product can alleviate that struggle. How can your sales copy motivate them to be better?

Saying Only What *Needs* to be Said

One major thing to keep in mind as you work through your product purpose and develop an audience definition is the vitality of distinguishing between what you do and what you need to talk about with your audience. People generally have limited attention spans. Therefore, one of the worst mistakes you can make is getting on a soapbox about yourself and the product instead of addressing what the target audience truly cares about. Knowing why the product exists is essential, but you should be able to summarize it in as few words as possible for your prospective audience to quickly and easily consume.

Remember, your sales copy should aim to appeal to what your audience members want to hear and what matters most to them instead of what matters most to you.

Implementing "Fear Factor"

One significant way to keep audience members engaged is by instilling an element of fear at all that could be at stake. By playing off the reader's fears, you are introducing the potential of suffering if they do not choose to invest in the product. To do this, you need to understand what your readers fear the most.

What contributes to their daily stress and keeps them up at night? In the case of the all-natural cleaning product audience, it is safe to assume that your audience fears the numerous risks to the mind and body from chemicals used in most household cleaners. They are likely afraid of themselves and their families becoming so poisoned by chemicals overtime that they develop a terrible disease.

Establishing Pain Points

Along the same lines of establishing a fear factor, you need to develop a pain point for your readers. What may be making it difficult for your audience to take the plunge into spending a little extra money on all-natural cleaning products? The pain point's primary goal is to make your audience feel seen by acknowledging what it is that makes it difficult for them to invest in this new product. In the household cleaner's case, the pain point may be that all-natural products are more expensive or do not work.

You can play into this pain point by comparing the results of your product to a name brand product that has a lot of chemicals but works great, as well as comparing it to another all-natural product that may leave behind residue or have an unpleasant odor or consistency. In establishing this comparison, you are telling your audience, "I know you are probably worried about this, so I'm going to show you that there is no need to worry." You can claim that an extra dollar or two now is worth thousands of dollars in potential medical bills later in terms of the financial pain point.

Maintaining Conversational Tone

Although you will write your sales copy from a place of urgency, it is still essential to maintain a conversational tone with your readers. Consider each reader as your friend, and speak to them as if you have known them forever. Take time to establish the common ground between yourself and your audience members, creating a sense of relatability and comfort. One of the best ways to maintain this conversational tone is by being transparent.

Acknowledge that you have experienced the same doubts, frustrations, and worries as your audience and that you know how it feels. As you speak to them, talk to them from the position of a friend who truly has their best interest at heart. Additionally, make sure to communicate the "secret language" of your audience. This will further your point and make your audience members feel like you and almost the same people. This is incredibly important in persuading the audience members to purchase your product, as people are more likely to trust the advice of those they like and relate to.

Conducting User Surveys

People and industries are always changing, and as a result, it can be challenging to keep track and make sure your sales copies advertise products that are aligned with what people want. One way to stay on top of understanding your audience and what they want is to conduct regular user surveys. The questions should be short, to the point, and simple to complete while also being intentional. You should draft each item with a clear idea of what you hope to learn about your audience demographics. You can use social media as a tool for audience engagement by creating posts that ask your audience to tell you more about themselves. What do they struggle with daily? What do they value most? What are their favorite pastimes? What products do they wish they had, and what holds them back from having those products?

Twitter and Instagram polls are just a few of the options available for surveying your audience via social media. Another thing to remember with social media is the importance of responding to comments and messages, get involved with conversations within your niche, and always making a conscious effort to learn more about your audience.

Conducting Individual Interviews

Another method for ensuring you're on track with understanding your audience is by reaching out individually to a few dedicated social media followers, readers, or members of your niche to conduct a personal interview. Show these people how much their feedback and perspective matters to you, and be sure to ask them a lot of questions and be open to their answers.

Avoiding Common Assumptions

When it comes to an understanding of your audience, there are a few assumptions that you should strive to avoid. Making false assumptions about your audience is one of the worst mistakes that can be made in sales copywriting because it either gives your audience the impression that they don't know enough to keep up or that you are criticizing them for where they are at. People do not respond well to either of these feelings, and if your content makes them feel this way, they will abandon it without a second thought.

First Assumption to Avoid: Assuming your Audience Cares

The first assumption you should strive to avoid is that your audience cares about your product. You must remind yourself that the people you are appealing to have vast lives beyond the context of reading what you write about a product, and there are things that are of much higher priority to them. Your audience members' loved ones and their interests are far more important to them than connecting with any brand. You must approach your sales copywriting either with the assumption that your audience does *not* care about your brand and that you must find a way to make them care, or better yet, with no assumptions at all. If you assume that your audience members care about your brand and are only going to continue to care more, you will be drastically misguided and will therefore lose readers as quickly as they arrive.

Second Assumption to Avoid: Assuming your Audience is Exactly Like You

A second assumption to avoid is that your audience is exactly like you. Although you likely share many similarities with your audience members and value many of the same things, you are different people with different personalities and goals. The best sales copywriters write from the influence of personal experience and strong data instead of preconceived notions about who their audience is. As a sales copywriter, you should always operate under the assumption that you have more to learn about your audience.

Third Assumption to Avoid: Assuming the Possession of Knowledge or Jargon

Lastly, it would be best if you strived to avoid assuming that your audience possesses the same knowledge and jargon as you do. Because you and your audience are different people with different experiences, you cannot assume that you know the same things. In some cases, they will be more knowledgeable than you, and in other cases, you will be more familiar. More than this, however, is the fact that you both hold knowledge in different areas. It is important to remember that one of the driving forces for engaging with content is the desire to expand one's experience on a particular topic.

Therefore, it is essential to use clear, simple language that can be understood by most readers. It is not a good idea to use industry jargon, as this is almost sure to create a stumbling block for new readers and make them feel that their knowledge is inadequate. If you do use industry jargon, you should present it as if it is the first time the reader has seen it. If you are wondering which details you should include in establishing a piece of baseline knowledge for readers, it is better to use more information than less. This is important even if you are writing about something that you assume everyone knows, as the reality is, they likely do not. You cannot assume your audience is an expert in the content you are writing about, or you will run the risk of losing them.

Persuading Reader Action

The primary goal of the sales page is to persuade the reader to do what you are urging them to do (whether that is signing up for a course, purchasing a product, etc.) The purpose behind a sales page is to influence your audience to make a decision you want. When people finish reading your sales page, they will make their own decision about whether or not they wish to buy your product or take your course. No matter what you are trying to convince the audience to do, the sales pitch must maintain the goal of persuasion from start to finish.

Types of Sales Pages

There are options for text only, video only, or combination pages for creating a sales page. In this guide, we will focus mostly on the text-only sales page, in which all of the content is written in text.

It is especially crucial with text-only sales pages to include images and visual aids which build the text, create a sense of visual appeal, and make the reader feel more engaged with the content. If you choose to do a sales page that is a combination of text and video, you can simply create a video portion that summarizes the written content.

Understanding Audience Motivations

In Chapter 1, you learned how to identify your target audience. In doing this, you understood the most likely people to be interested in what you have to offer. Once again, although necessary demographic information is helpful, it should not be the primary focus.

What you need to understand is what motivates your audience, what they struggle with, what pain they strive to avoid, or the pleasure they strive to bring into their lives. Ultimately, you must understand why they would benefit from what you have to offer. To make sales, you must make people feel that they are investing in themselves and what they can accomplish.

Defining Audience Benefits

When it comes to writing a sales page, one of the biggest questions you should expect your audience to ask is, "What's in it for me?" You must identify the aspects of your product, course, etc. that would benefit your audience. What can you help them with? Are you offering to improve their health, relationship status, career advancement, the general quality of life? Before you begin writing your sales page, it is a good idea to sit down with a pen and paper and answer these questions. You must be able to clearly define how your audience can benefit from making this particular investment.

Creating Compelling Content

The content you write on your sales page is crucial to determining whether you will succeed in making sales. The content must be compelling, and there is a specific order you should follow to keep the audience on track as they read it.

Element 1: Capturing Headline

The first element of an effective sales page is a capturing headline. This headline should be compelling and should immediately draw your audience to the page. The purpose of the headline is to grab the audience's attention and make them want to find out what happens next. The introduction's goal is not to introduce the course itself but rather to inflict interest in your reader and inspire them to keep reading.

Element 2: Engaging Opening Narrative

The following element of an effective sales page is the opening narrative. This is used to introduce the reader's problem and demonstrate empathy towards their struggles or frustrations. This is an excellent place to speak to your own experience, especially if you have struggled with the same things your reader is now struggling with. By telling the story of your struggles and reminding your reader of the risks of not solving the problem at hand, you build a healthy transition into the proposal of a solution (which is inevitably to purchase your product, course, etc.) Readers will be much more likely to make this investment if they feel seen and understood by someone who has faced the same struggles as them. They will be more trusting if they can refer to the story you tell and see how the product or course can help overcome the issue at hand. Ultimately, it will be the prospect of transformation and growth that will inspire someone to make the purchase.

Element 3: Introducing Logistics

In writing a sales page, you must assume that the solution to your reader's problem is to purchase the content you are advertising. This is the part of the page where you begin to introduce the logistics of the product, course, etc. and make the reader aware of the range of benefits. As you describe your work, course, etc. ask yourself which particular services can apply to your reader's lives. How will they benefit from this? What will they learn? How will their life improve as a result?

Element 4: Utilizing Bulleted Lists

One of the best ways to describe the benefits of what you have to offer is using a bulleted list. A good number of benefits to list on your sales page is 5-10. To develop this list, consider the most prominent benefits of taking the course. Bulleted lists are more visual and more comfortable to read than a block of text. Therefore, they are very useful for grabbing the attention of people who may be reading your sales page in a hurry or who have trouble focusing. You need to be bold and to the point in presenting the significant benefits of your product, course, etc. and a bulleted list is an excellent way to do that.

Element 5: Providing Testimonials

Another step to the process of drafting your sales page is to provide testimonials for social proof. Once you have established the problem and the solution, you need to back up your claims using the opinions of people other than yourself. In doing this, you can help your reader feel assured that the course, product, etc. will benefit them and that the developer is not only feeding them biased information. Testimonials are the third-party proof and credibility that you need to provide this assurance to the readers.

By sharing the stories of other people who have used this product, taken this course, etc., you demonstrate that the claims you make about the product are valid and that the reader's life will indeed improve due to making this investment. Reach out to people who have taken your course or purchased your product before and ask them to provide written or video reviews/testimonials. Testimonials are most potent when you give the name and title of the person and an image of them, if possible, to increase the human factor. Make sure that any testimonial you use is legitimate; never make up a testimonial. If you are just getting started and haven't had enough clients or built up enough of a community to gather testimonials, consider offering a free trial to several people in exchange for their testimonials or reviews.

Element 6: Providing a Credible Biography

Another element along the lines of credibility is to provide a biography of yourself, which demonstrates your credibility. In the case of the all-natural cleaning product, you could give some background into your research of various cleaning chemicals and the implications on the human body. You may also provide your narrative of trying several products before finally finding the one that worked best. In this case, your trial and error can save the reader from having to go through all that trouble by leading them to the "best choice" the first time. If you are teaching a course, your instructor biography is where you can showcase what makes you credible as an instructor and which positive results you will lead your students towards. Ultimately, your instructor bio should serve to prove to your reader that you have the knowledge and expertise required to guide them in the right direction.

Element 7: Addressing Concerns with an FAQ

Although it is not a requirement, including an FAQ section can help increase levels of engagement and interest in your sales page. This gives you a space to address the reader's concerns, questions, and objections when they see that someone else has already brought it to the table and had it clarified. You can design these questions yourself by deciding 5-10 questions you imagine would be most commonly asked about your course. If you can't come up with enough questions, you can use social media to host a webinar or post a polling option for your followers to respond with their problems.

Element 8: Providing Risk Reversal

When people choose to invest time, money, and energy into a particular product or service, they will feel a certain degree of uncertainty. As they strive to make the right decision, they will inevitably ask themselves what will happen if they are unhappy with the product or service results. Will they get compensated for their disappointment? If so, what kind of compensation will they receive? This is where the risk reversal (also known as the satisfaction guarantee) portion of the sales page comes in. In this portion, you have to be able to address any concerns or potential regrets of your potential buyers, especially those who do not know you in person and have had no experience with your products or services. One common tactic for risk reversal is offering a full refund within a certain period.

In most cases, this period to receive 100% money back is within 30 days. By providing this option, readers no longer feel the stress of a risk that goes along with buying a product or service they don't know a lot about. In providing this full refund option, you are also giving credibility by saying that you are so sure of the benefits you are willing to give people all of their money back if they don't have that experience. Although some people may take advantage of this refund policy, it will more than balance out because of the number of customers you will gain due to increased comfort levels through a money-back guarantee.

Element 9: Leaving an Impression with Postscript

The P.S. or Postscript section of your sales page is optional but highly recommended, especially to maintain the conversational tone discussed in chapter one. On the sales page, the P.S. takes on the form of a single paragraph at the end of the completed letter. The P.S. summarizes the entire sales letter's main points as one last reminder to the reader about what is available to them and why they should care. This section is crucial for capturing the attention of people who skim through sales pages and just want to reach the end. The P.S. should contain a brief recap of what you discussed, as well as a personal note that will stick with the reader and inspire them to take the next step.

Chapter 3: Step 3 - Telling a Story

When it comes to writing a sales copy, many people do not consider other creative writing elements as factors of the process. Many people who write successful sales copies are equipped with the talent of storytelling, so much so that it could be called the secret power of the most successful sales copywriters.

Because storytelling holds enough power to create such lasting impacts on the world, it is no wonder that the art of storytelling can be an incredibly useful tactic when it comes to writing sales copies. No one enjoys being sold to, but everyone enjoys a good story. By telling a story in the sales copies you write, you will build connections with your customers, allow them to engage with the product or service being advertised honestly, and inspire them to react.

Elements of Storytelling

Every meaningful story has a character, a conflict, and a resolution. In other words, the reader must be introduced to what the protagonist wants, what is standing in their way of obtaining it, and how their life will change if they do or do not obtain it. These same elements should be applied to the story you tell when writing a sales copy. There are several significant elements to telling a good story in your sales copy, which are as follows: introduce a character with a problem, a guide with a plan to overcome that problem, a final call to action, an idea of what can happen if the reader chooses to buy the product or service, as well as what is at stake for them if they decide not to.

Making the Customer a Hero

Every good story has a main character who serves as the protagonist, or hero, of the story. The plot of the story revolves around this character and their particular goals. To begin writing your customer into the storyline of a sales copy, you must make your customer the hero. Identify the customer's goals-- what is it that they want? Your customer is the protagonist in this story, and the rest of the story revolves around them and the choice they make. Everyone is the hero of their own story, and everyone has goals they strive to achieve in life. In general, every human being seeks to achieve something they don't have and positively transform their lives.

Additionally, every human being knows what it is like to face obstacles on the road to where we want to be. When these obstacles arise, the natural human response is to look for guidance or assistance to help overcome those obstacles to reach our goals. In the case of a sales copy, this assistance to overcoming obstacles comes in the form of the product or service. Your sales copy should aim to show the customer how this product will meet their needs and help them accomplish their goals. One of the worst mistakes a sales copywriter can make is to assume that the product or service is the hero, not the guide. It is crucial to remember that the customer is the hero; the product or service being advised is simply the guide the protagonist can take advantage of to improve their lives and overcome their challenges.

Playing on Basic Human Needs

If you are wondering what to use to motivate potential customers as the characters in their own stories, look for a reference to the basic survival needs that all humans have. The first of these is to conserve time. In the case of the all-natural cleaner, you could appeal to this human need by stating that the cleaner "Works efficiently, making your surfaces sparkling clean with just a quick spray and wipe down." The second motivation is building social networks and gaining status within those networks.

To appeal to this need, you could say something such as "Purchasing ShiningDay All-Purpose Cleaner for your home is the next step you can take as a member of the community of health and environmental warriors." This presents the idea of gaining status as a member of this community, which is rallied around a particular cause. Next is the conservation of financial resources. Especially in the case of more expensive products, it is your job to show readers why this purchase is better for them financially in the long run.

For this example, you could say: "The chemicals in everyday all-purpose cleaners have been proven to increase the risk of cancer, which costs people thousands of dollars in medical bills. Choose ShiningDay today, and save the costs of medical bills later." Another common need to play into is the need for the accumulation of resources. Human beings are wired to survive, and therefore, the idea of being deprived of anything is terrifying. One way to do this regarding the ShiningDay cleaner would be to say, "We only have one chance at a healthy body, and one chance at a healthy planet. Decide to preserve both today." The next common need is the need to find meaning in our lives and the decisions we make.

One way to do it in this example would be to say, "When it comes to keeping our bodies and planets safe, every person has a role to play. There is no room to sit by and wait for someone else to take action." This inspires readers to take the plunge on their own to pursue purpose and live the best life they can. By that same token, most human beings have the desire to give. Saying something along the lines of: "Purchasing ShiningDay all-natural cleaner today is the first step you can take to give back to your body and Mother Earth for all they have done for you."

Identifying Conflict

Another crucial element of storytelling is to identify the conflict. In sales copywriting, this conflict is the problem your customer's faces, and it should serve as the antagonist of the story. The villain can be a person, object, or concept, but it must possess human characteristics to activate the reader's appropriate response. In the case of the ShiningDay all-purpose cleaner, the "villain" of the story could be the chemicals of typical all-purpose cleaners that have been proven to lead to cancer. Some of the human characteristics you can apply to these chemicals are "ravaging the human body," "stripping people of financial resources," etc.

When it comes to conflict, there are two sides to the coin: internal and external conflict. External conflict is the more obvious of the two, such as a person needing to keep their house clean while also avoiding chemicals but having trouble with the efficiency of every all-natural cleaner they have tried. The internal problem, however, is the force that is profoundly driving the customer.

In this example, it can be assumed that a customer's deep driving force is the desire to protect themselves and their families from getting sick. Another example of an internal problem that could be adopted concerning the scenario is that the person knows the environment is dying and wants to do what they can to protect it. When you address the internal problem, you are appealing to your customer's deepest motivations and addressing what truly matters to them. As a sales copywriter, you must know how to give attention to both internal and external problems. In doing this, you will manage to effectively turn your customer's issues into the villain of the story, which will, in turn, motivate them to the action of buying the product or service.

Revealing the Guide

The resolution of a good story comes after the character has been represented. The reader is on the edge of their seat, wondering if the character will manage to overcome the conflict they face. In the resolution, some sort of guide appears to reveal to the character how they can overcome the challenges they face and achieve their goal. In a sales copy, the guide is the product or service being advertised. The story itself is not about the guide; it is about the character and their quest to reach their goal. The product or service is simply a tool they used to help them overcome their challenges and get the place they were trying to go. Therefore, it is imperative not to allow your product or service to take the spotlight away from the customer and their ultimate goals.

Fostering Empathy

As the sales copywriter who introduces the reader to the product or service, it is your job to guide them on their decision journey. You must establish a presence as someone who has all the information the reader needs to reach their goals. When it comes to the guide (your product or service), two qualities must be present.

The first of these is empathy, which provides an understanding of the customer's problem. People will not respond to suggestions if they do not feel that what they are dealing with is fully understood, and they will not accept guidance unless they feel truly seen. As a sales copywriter, it is your job to build this sense of empathy by detailing your understanding of the problem your customer is facing and the complicated emotions they are likely experiencing as a result.

Establishing Authority

The second quality you must present in your product or service as the story guide is authority. You have to show your customer why they should trust you and the solution you offer to their problem. One of the best ways to establish authority is through the use of testimonials. By using testimonials, readers can refer to the experiences of others. If they see that many people have written raving reviews about a particular product or service and that all the proclaimed benefits are real, they will be much more comfortable taking the jump themselves. Another way to express authority is by providing credible sources where information has been drawn from, as well as where the advice or expertise from your product or service development team has been featured. The final tactic for establishing authority is through personal narrative.

You can establish a sense of relatability with the reader by showing them that you have been in their shoes, struggling, and failing to reach the same goals they are trying to achieve. An example of this would be to describe your battle to find the household cleaner that upheld your values of health and environmental protection while also being practical and easy to use.

Presenting a Plan

After you have established a sense of empathy and authority in your guide (the product or service), you must provide your reader with a plan for how to succeed. What are the steps that will take the reader to where they want to go? In the case of the ShiningDay cleaner, perhaps the plan would look something like: "Buy your first bottle risk-free today, and begin paving your way to a cleaner future, one spritz at a time."

Providing a Clear Purpose

In every good story, the protagonist is called to take action beyond the scope of what they had tried before. The hero does not take this action independently; instead, there must be another person or force that urges them to do so. This is where the guide comes in. The story's guide is the external force that causes the protagonist to take a necessary next step into overcoming their barriers and achieving their goals. People need a purposeful reason as to why they should take this next step in their journey and a clear explanation of what will happen once they do. The call to action needs to be clear and should be repeated several times throughout the sales copy.

Explaining What's at Stake

According to the Negativity Bias, the prospect of a positive impact is less likely to influence human behavior than the possibility of a negative impact. Therefore, merely providing the positive effects that can occur if your reader purchases this product or service is not enough. To accomplish your goals with storytelling in sales copywriting, you must present both what will happen if the customer does take the action you are suggesting and what will happen if they do not. It is essential to show your reader what is at stake. In the example with the ShiningDay cleaner, what is at stake is the reader's health and their family and the preservation of the only planet that can support human life. To write a story with stakes, there must also be a threat of failure to motivate the reader further. As a writer, it is your job to establish these stakes using dramatic tension.

It is a good idea to write about the consequences in a way that inflicts some fear and urgency in your reader by showing them how neglecting this call to action would fail. Make it clear to the reader what could go wrong if they don't take action. Your goal should be to make your reader think that if they do not try ShiningDay cleaner, they are putting the health of themselves, their family, and the environment at dire risk, which will end in calamity. Paint the picture of the cost of not buying your product or service. Ask your reader to imagine themselves in the future, living in a world where their health, the health of a loved one, or the health of the planet has been jeopardized to the point of no return.

Writing the Triumph

The last element of storytelling in sales copywriting is when the hero overcomes the obstacles, triumphs over the villain, and ends up on top. At this point, the protagonist overcomes the problem, which was identified at the start of the story. After the protagonist has overcome this problem, their life becomes better than it ever could have been before.

Every human being has the desire to end up somewhere better than where they are right now, and you must play into that desire in the sales copies you write. What elements of your reader's lives will be better after they have bought the product or service? What feelings will they have that they don't currently have? What will a day in their life look like? How will they rise in status? Paint a picture for the reader of how much joy and success they will have at the end of their journey once they have chosen to invest in your product or service. Help them envision their future so clearly that they cannot imagine living any longer without your product or service. It is crucial to detail every success your reader can expect in their new and better life.

Chapter 4: Step 4 - Developing your Rebuttal

As mentioned earlier, nobody enjoys being sold to. As a sales copywriter, you can expect that it will be challenging to hold people's interest long enough for them to finish reading, and even if you do, prospective customers will be sure to pose objections. Any time you try to convince a person to do something, they will naturally have some questions and concerns. Luckily, sales objections offer a unique opportunity for you to use the power of rebuttal to capture the audience's attention and respect and take the results of their reading into your own hands.

Because sales copies are written and do not occur as a conversational give-and-take, you must think hypothetically about the reader's opposition to what you are proposing. The best way to keep readers engaged even when they become skeptical is to redirect them when doubts arise. Throughout the sales copy, you must assume doubts the reader has and speak to those doubts in a way that keeps the reader engaged and steers the conversation away from their objection and towards the ultimate goal.

Redirection Strategies

If a reader begins to think to themselves, "This cleaner is too expensive, there is no way I can afford it," your job is to redirect that thinking. One method of doing this is to make the reader think of something else they spend money on. You can make a statement like: "You may be thinking to yourself, 'I can't afford these fancy all-natural cleaning products.' This concern is entirely understandable, as it does indeed cost more to make high-quality cleaning products with high-quality ingredients.

That said, I would encourage you to think about the cost of medical bills. A few extra dollars a month for an all-natural cleaner is worth the thousands of dollars and potentially years of life you can save by making this simple investment in the health of your loved ones and yourself."

Redirection is useful because it acknowledges the validity of the reader's concerns while simultaneously regaining control of the narrative and giving the reader something to think about as the proposal draws to a close. It brings up additional challenges and things to think about, such as all the money lost on medical bills if a person gets cancer from the chemicals in their current household cleaners. It is often the perspective offered in the rebuttal, which serves as the final selling point for a product or service.

Following the Formula

When it comes to developing a sales rebuttal, a specific formula can be applied in nearly every situation. This formula begins with an acknowledgment of the problem. Acknowledgment is important because it shows the reader that you are willing to meet them where they are and truly see their concerns. From here, the formula introduces redirection by either asking a question of the reader or introducing a value statement. Redirection is the turning point of the conversation, which shifts control away from the skeptical reader and back to yourself and the proposal at hand. The question comes next and should serve to qualify the customer and create a connection between your product or service's benefit concerning a pain point in the reader's life. This is used in the example by introducing the reader's prospect of losing someone they love due to the chemicals in a daily household cleaner or losing money to pay for failing health. The question is most useful when you are dealing with a profoundly skeptical customer who is not easy to convince.

On the other hand, a value statement comes in when things are farther underway, and the reader has begun to develop a more profound interest. The value statement should introduce the positive aspects of purchasing this product or service and serve as positive reinforcement for the interest that already exists.

As you move into the later stages of the sales copy, and thus, the reader's potential objections, you should introduce how you are different from other competitors in your industry. What sets you apart and makes you unique, regardless of having potentially similar goals to other product or service providers? In the case of the ShiningDay cleaner, perhaps it has a better scent, more solution in the bottle for the price leaves behind a less sticky residue doesn't need as much solution to do its job, etc.

Things to Avoid

There are several things to avoid when it comes to developing a rebuttal. The first thing to avoid is being defensive to objections the reader may have as they read your sales copy. Remember, it is normal for people to have questions and concerns, especially regarding how they spend their money. It is essential not to be on the defense when you present your objections and certainly not to make the reader feel undermined or stupid. Another thing to avoid is focusing so much on the sale that you forget the customer's humanity reading the sales copy. Your focus should always be on the customer above anything else. Lastly, you should avoid launching a list of all the features of a product or a service at the reader without explaining the benefits or value of those features. If you only tell the reader what the features are and not why they make a difference, the reader will quickly become bored with the list and lose sight of what is essential.

Chapter 5: Step 5 - Exciting your Audience

When most people think of reading for enjoyment or entertainment, they are not thinking of sales copies. However, as we explored earlier in this guide, there is a much greater potential for audience engagement with sales copies than one might initially think. The most important way to do this is by generating feelings of excitement for your audience. By activating their emotions and making them excited, you can ensure that their motivation levels will be much higher, and they will be much more likely to take action. To yield this feeling of excitement in our readers, you should carefully select the language that is both contemporary and adheres to the goals of the product or service.

You must reflect the particular brand's overall tone and personality and create a high level of attraction for your target audience. As discussed in Chapter 1, you will be able to generate the most engaging sales copy if you are aware of your typical readers' persona. In knowing what makes your audience who they are, you will be able to approach them in a much more authentic way and make them feel comfortable and understood.

You should be aware of what your target audience generally agrees and disagrees with, and they should know very soon after they begin to read that this sales copy was written to appeal to them. Take time to write out the everyday things that they struggle with, what they aspire to, and what kinds of solutions would build an energy of excitement at the prospect of overcoming their challenges and reaching their goals. Once you have followed the tips in Chapter 1 of defining your target audience, you must learn how to keep them engaged with the content and excited to get involved.

Building Long-Term Relationships

A great way to foster excitement in your readers is by creating an environment of long-term relationships. Readers are much more likely to feel excited if they feel like they matter, they are essential, and they are on the same page as you are in terms of the product or service's mission. It is vital to make readers feel like an integral part of the community surrounding your product or service mission statement. Not only can this relationship-building increase levels of trust and likelihood that readers will buy the product or service, but it also shows them that you value and care about them as people. This often yields more significant profit growth over time, as the customer will continue to come purchase, advocate, and talk to their friends, family, co-workers, and followers about how much they love and support your product or service.

Proving the "Must-Haves"

Another way to increase your readers' excitement levels is by making your products or services into must-haves. One way to do this is by reiterating what distinguishes this particular product or service from all the others on the market.

A key element to making this distinguishment is by highlighting every advantage and valuable feature of the product or service that sets it apart. By highlighting these advantages, readers will see that you clearly understand the other products and services that exist in this market and that you have proven why yours is superior. If you do this correctly, your audience will not only understand the value of your product or service; they will feel they cannot live without it.

Weighing Out Features and Benefits

As you consider your product or service elements that are most exciting to other people, it's a good idea to ask yourself what makes *you* excited about it. One of the best ways to do this is by making a list of the best features and benefits of this product or service and how those things can change the reader's lives. While you want to avoid putting this list into the sales copy itself (remember, the goal should be to write about customer's problems and how they can find a solution), they can shape the way you frame the story.

When you pull features from the list to describe in the sales copy, be sure to add detailed descriptions of how those particular features are of use to your reader and their goals. It is important to start with features, then turn them into actionable benefits that can serve to solve your reader's problems and help them reach a higher state. In the case of ShiningDay, a feature may be that it contains a new jasmine and lemon scent, while a benefit may be that it keeps the home smelling fresh all day.

Developing a Unique Central Idea

Another critical element of generating audience excitement is to develop a unique and captivating central idea. The central idea should be the thing that sticks with readers after reading your sales copy and makes the purpose of your product or service feel important to them. This idea should provide a specific focus for your audience, expressed in the headline, and intertwined throughout the rest of the sales copy to keep the audience curious and emotionally invested.

There is nothing that dims audience excitement like a sales copy that drones on and on and becomes far too complicated to follow. You should use simple and engaging language that is straight to the point about addressing the customer's needs and desires and having a lasting benefit in their life. It is crucial to stay away from long sentences or extensive vocabulary that may cause your reader to become distracted from the content's central message. Readers should be able to understand what you're talking about immediately, without having to take time to try to figure out what is being discussed. It is vital to use colorful language and connect your content to things that matter to your audience and are familiar to them.

Using Your Imagination

Although it is essential to use simple, to the point language, there is a lot of room to use your imagination. Sales copywriting does not have to be bland or dry, and in fact, can provide an excellent opportunity to tap into your creative field. When you engage with your imaginative side, the sky becomes the limit in terms of how you can keep your readers engaged and persuade them to take the desired action. How can your product or service change their lives?

A great way to keep imagination and creativity alive is by using vivid, descriptive language. As you describe your product's benefits, mention details that will engage all of your reader's senses and immerse them in a full-body experience as they imagine the impact of your product or service on their life. If they imagine the fresh smell of lemon and jasmine lingering in their house all day, reminding them of a floral veranda near the beach, their senses will be pleasantly engaged, and they will be more likely to want to have the product.

Chapter 6: Step 6 - Defining a Call to Action

Earlier in the guide, we discussed the importance of developing a strong call to action. But what does that look like? There are several tactics for creating a powerful call to action, which will inspire your reader to purchase the product right away. When developing a call to action, it is essential not only to give the customer direction for what to do next but also how that action is going to benefit their lives. One of the best ways to do this is by providing a statistic or percentage, such as "By designing a product with all-natural ingredients to be used in place of common household cleaners, the risk of cancer is decreased by up to 50%."

In a world where people are always overwhelmed by things to do and places to be, your call to action must be strong enough to ensure that the reader's desire to purchase the product or service does not become lost in the shuffle of their life. It is an excellent idea to offer options like a wish list or links to learn more so that the reader can further their exciting engagement with the product and follow through on their eventual purchase. By offering things that readers can act on and come back to later, you lessen the risk of a reader intending to take action and then forgetting to do so.

Developing a Button

If you are tying your call to action to a button on a webpage, the button should be brightly colored, flashy, and impossible to miss. You need to ensure that the button sticks out from the rest of the page by being in a contrasting color, precisely one with some relationship with your product or service's logo or the general atmosphere.

Let's consider an online sales copy for the ShiningDay all-purpose cleaner.

Imagine that the company logo is a nature scene, with the sun shining brightly in a clear blue sky over a green field. In an online sales copy for ShiningDay, you could direct the reader to take a low-stakes action such as entering their email address, or a higher stakes action like choosing the first item to add to their cart. You could also create a "package" of some kind, in which the participant can spend $30 and get three items free, for example. Either way, the call-to-action button should stick out from the black and white of the rest of the page, preferably utilizing colors from the logo like yellow, bright blue, or green.

Providing Clarity

A strong call to action should leave no room for questions about what the reader needs to do next. It should spell out exactly what action they need to take and should leave no room for doubt or question. Your readers are looking for clarity—they need to know precisely what is being asked of them. That said, it is essential not to overwhelm readers by providing multiple calls to action. A single call to action is more than sufficient, and you are much more likely to see the desired results that way. Focus on a single action that will benefit both the potential customer and yourself, and allow all secondary benefits to fall into the background. Take the opportunity to stress this action multiple times throughout the sales copy, at least once in the proposal's body, and again in conclusion. If you can include an actionable step, such as a button or a link, this will further the ability to direct your readers to action.

"Sign Up Now" Call to Action

There are several interactable calls to action you can include in the sales copies you write. The first is the "Sign Up Now" call to action, which is generally used for business proposals when you are asking a customer to form a mutually beneficial business relationship. This approach strongly urges the reader to take a particular action and leaves them little space to back out. In the case of the ShiningDay cleaner, the "Sign Up Now" call to action could be used in asking a similar company, perhaps one that focused on creating all-natural, non-toxic laundry detergent, or trash bags out of recycled materials, to partner with ShiningDay.

"Join Our Mailing List" Call to Action

The second option is the "Join Our Mailing List": option, which is used when sending proposals to businesses or individuals you are not familiar with. This method is a less direct but often more widespread approach. In many cases, sales copies with a call to action like this can be sent out to many people, even those beyond the target audience who are not as likely to be interested. Although this method does not guarantee as many sales, it is a quick and easy way to get your proposal out in the world and see what happens.

You can attach forms to these mailing lists which prospective customers can fill out, and from which you can follow up with at a later date. An example of how this could be used with ShiningDay would be to send ads to people whose social media interests revolve around health, environmentalism, or both. Buttons that invite members to get on the email list, a low-stakes option that can give rise to higher stakes involvement, are great ideas. These options are great to include on company webpages for readers who are clicking around and exploring the page but are not yet ready to make a broader commitment.

"Watch the Video" Call to Action

Another option is a "Watch the Video" call to action, which is often sent to existing customers. This tactic is the "nurturing" call to action, which works to deepen existing customer relationships. In nurturing the connections that already exist with past customers, you can increase customer loyalty and inspire them to reach out to their friends. This approach gives customers who feel that they are starting to know you, but need to know a little more, the opportunity to learn more and understand the fact that your product or service is superior. In the ShiningDay example, this might be sent out to previous clients to say, "ShiningDay has a brand-new scent, and as our valued customer, you're the first one to see it! Let us know what you think."

Chapter 7: Step 7 - Setting your Sales Copy Apart

We live in a society where people are regularly buying and selling, trying to figure out the new best product to buy to fit their needs, or in the case of product or service developers, the new best product or service that will make their company successful. As a sales copywriter, you have your work cut out for you to prove the excellence of your product or service and get readers to follow through with the desired actions. Several things help set your sales copy apart from the norm.

Conducting Thorough Research

The first thing to keep in mind is the importance of conducting thorough research. The better you know your subject matter about the item you're trying to sell, the higher your chances are of successfully selling it. You need to demonstrate that you have an intricate understanding of the market and the offerings of your competitors and provide research and evidence to back up any claims you make about what sets your product or service apart.

To prove what makes your offer special, you have to dedicate a lot of time to dig through all of the similarities between your product and its competitors until you finally hit the jackpot of what sets it apart. Once you have identified what qualities make your product or service unique, dig deeper, researching until you have plenty of evidence to present to your audience about what makes your product or service superior to the rest.

Using Personal Narrative

Another tool you can use to your advantage in developing a sales copy is the use of your own back story or personal narrative. The vulnerability expressed in sharing your own story will not only gain you the trust of potential customers, but it will also help convey important lessons and compel them to act sooner than you did so they can start living a better life. To tie this element of narrative into your writing, think of a few stories from the past which relate to the issue at hand. These stories can also come from other customers, so long as you have received permission. In the ShiningDay cleaner's case, the sales copywriter might share a story about how she was trying to make the shift to all-natural cleaners in her house but was dealing with the frustrations of cost and effectiveness until she found ShiningDay.

Creating Eye-Catching Subject Lines

When you are a sales copywriter, the last thing on earth that you can afford to be is boring. Eye-catching subject lines are one of the best ways to prove that you are exiting and intriguing, and these are the things that will ultimately draw people to keep reading. The subject line is often the first thing a reader will see, and therefore, you must be able to frame it just right to capture their attention and maintain it.

One way to capture and keep the reader's attention is by posing a question that will draw them in. In the ShiningDay example, you could say something like, "Did you know that at least 30% of all cancer cases in the United States are related to harmful chemicals found in everyday household cleaners?" A second option is to create a comparative subject line that poses your product or service directly against a competitor, such as "See how ShiningDay all-purpose cleaning products are superior to all other products in the all-natural cleaning product industry."

Another tactic is to make a numbered list of reasons why consumers should purchase your product or service. An example of this would be "11 Reasons Why You Should Purchase ShiningDay All-Natural All-Purpose Cleaner Today." Customers tend to be drawn to numbered lists because they can count on the concise, comprehensive content, which is both informative and easy to follow. Numbers and headlines with each number are beneficial in directing the reader's eyes and knowing what they need to know from the piece of content.

Keeping it Simple

Another major tip for sales copywriting is not to overcomplicate things. We have already discussed the importance of using language that is straight and to the point. To persuade an audience to do what you want, you must provide information in small, precise increments that are easy to follow. Run-on sentences and complex ideas surrounding why people should buy from you will not serve you well in the long run.

Keep your language short, engaging, and full of catchy adjectives. Allow yourself to tie emotion into your words and phrases to increase the level of emotional connection readers feel to your product or service. Be sure to maintain transparent communication modes that do not become cluttered with too many words or hard to grasp concepts.

Presenting a Sense of Urgency

After you have explained the benefits of your product or service and created a connection with the client, you must present a sense of urgency. As the reader finishes the sales copy, they should feel like this is something they have to accomplish right now or lose the opportunity. Time-sensitive language such as "today," "now," "limited time," or "right away" are all great for making the reader feel like they do not have a lot of time before they will need to act. It is crucial to make the reader aware of the regret they will have if they fail to follow the proposed solutions as soon as possible.

Highlighting the Benefits

Remember, it is important to stay away from droning on about features. Focus instead on the ways this product can benefit your client's lives. In the case of the ShiningDay cleaner, it is a good idea to highlight the benefits like "Smells amazing," "removes all tough stains," "contains no toxins," or "lasts for months."

These phrases all connect with human issues, like efficiency, preservation of health, saving money, and sensory pleasures. The reader is looking for how this product will benefit them, and you have to be sure to give that to them in your description. The benefit of all of these features provide is the real value proposition. After you have drawn their attention by describing the elements, you may launch into the fact that folks only have a limited time making their first purchase.

Prioritizing Reader's Needs

Lastly, you must remember that your job as a sales copywriter is to benefit both yourself and the other party. Although your selling needs are essential, you must focus on your readers' needs before your agenda. You must make it clear in your sales copy that you are setting your readers up for success in the future, even beyond this moment.

Your goal is to do everything in your power to prove to readers that this product or service is the thing that is going to change their life forever.

Conclusion

When you started this guide, you likely had a product or service you were interested in advertising through content writing, and you had the desire to set yourself apart in the sales copywriting industry. You were likely aware of all that is at stake in sales copywriting, especially considering our high-consuming society and the increased use of mediums like blogs, webpages, and social media.

Throughout the guide, you were provided with the sales copywriting the process's ins and outs, from how to determine your audience and how to keep engagement levels high to market yourself through your initial sales page. You learned audience appeal tactics, maintaining attention, directing the future course of action, and addressing common questions and concerns to develop your credibility further and reassure your audience. You became aware of the most common mistakes to avoid, such as being overly complicated, lacking imagination, or making the process too much about your own goals and not enough about the reader.

You discovered the importance of understanding and appealing to your audience, explaining what is at stake, avoiding faulty assumptions, developing an easy-to-follow structure, inciting emotion and excitement, and pushing back on common arguments through the formulation of strong rebuttals and tactics of making the reader feel seen. You came to understand the secrets of sales copy organization and structure, as well as the language that will spark the reader's interest and inspire them to act.

At the end of the guide, you were provided with the tips that set excellent sales copywriters apart from all the rest. These tips will help you advance from amateur sales copywriter in no time, and your sales are sure to go up as a result.

This guide has helped you discover how to capture and maintain reader engagement and increase levels of excitement and inspiration towards action in readers. This guide is sure to serve as your toolbox throughout your sales copywriting journey to guide your every move.

More by Jaiden Pemton

Discover all books from the Creative Writing Series by Jaiden Pemton at:

<u>bit.ly/jaiden-pemton</u>

Book 1: *How to Write Fiction*

Book 2: *How to Tell a Story*

Book 3: *How to Write a Screenplay*

Book 4: *How to Write Sales Copy*

Book 5: *How to Edit Writing*

Book 6: *How to Self-Publish*

Book 7: *How to Write Non-Fiction*

Book 8: *How to Write Content*

Themed book bundles available at discounted prices:

<u>bit.ly/jaiden-pemton</u>

9 798869 083791